Love is in the Air

Published by Marfa House

Copyright 2017

Marfa House
Marfa, Texas

Marfa House
Marfa, Texas

Love is in the Air
Published by Marfa House

This book is a work of fiction. With the exception of recognized historical figures, the characters in this novel are fictional. Any resemblance to actual persons, living or dead, is purely coincidental.

All Rights Reserved

Copyright 2017
1st Edition

In accordance with the U.S. Copyright Act of 1976, the scanning, uploading, and electronic sharing of any part of this book without the permission of the publisher constitute unlawful piracy and theft of the author's intellectual property. If you would like permission to use this author's material work other than for reviews, prior written permission must be obtained by contacting the publisher. Thank you for your support of the author's rights.

This book is licensed for your personal enjoyment only. This book may not be re-sold or given away to other people. If you would like to share this book with another person, please purchase an additional copy for each recipient. If you're reading this book and did not purchase it, or it was not purchased for your use only, then please purchase your own copy. Thank you for respecting the hard work of this author.

ISBN: 978-1-946072-54-2

Dedication

For all those who have ever found love in the darkness. For all those who have ever found love at random times with their soulmates. This book is for you; let your love shine through like the beacon it was meant to be.

Love Without Limit

By Delfin Espinosa

The love of a soul mate will last forever
if you can see that you will be clever.
It is a love without limit
because it comes from the spirit.
A love that comes from the heart
it creates a tremendous spark.
A love that will wash over the pain
it will remove every stain.
It is a love that will mend the soul
and remove the tears that have taken their toll.
When you find a soul mates love hold on tight
for it is indeed a beautiful sight.

Anniel
By Kimberly M. Heindorf

My dog panted happily next to me as we made our way to my fruit garden. My grandparents were coming to visit this weekend, and mom had asked that I make some strawberry tarts for them. I ruffled Honey's large black and white head and I watched as her ears flopped back and forth.

Honey gave a bark and took off running. Gripping my basket tighter, I chased after her.

"Honey?" I called.

"Aw! You gave me a pet name? That's so nice, darling!" A voice called back.

I nearly growled at the sight of Elon. He was kneeling in the middle of my patch rubbing my dog, who was on her back bearing her belly. The traitor.

"What are you doing here?" I grumbled, crossing my arms over my chest.

"Your mom called me to help you with the strawberries. Said you'd need more than usual because my family is coming over this weekend."

I nearly groaned out loud.

Our families were friends since forever. Literally forever. As two of the longest lines of cupids, we found a way to work alongside one another to bring people together.

Every person had a red string that came from their heart, but showed on their wrist and it entwined with another's. It was our job to find these matching strings and pull it to make the couple come together.

The only kind of "humans" that didn't have the strings was cupids. We usually end up with other cupids. It's against the Cupid's Codex to have relations with humans who have red strings. It was a cupid's sole duty to bring people together, not keep them apart.

We had family scattered all across the states and some family in a building in New York City that found couples online and magically brought them together. That's where I wanted to end up after high school. But for now I'm stuck matching high school sweethearts with Elon.

He was decent, but he was one of those people I could only take small doses of. As with everyone else. At least that's what I keep telling myself. I think I really liked the idea of New York because I would be left alone for the most part. Maybe then I could pull myself together.

"Fine, start pulling the weeds," I said.

"Yes, dear."

I rolled my eyes and bent down to started plucking the strawberries.

It didn't take us long to finish. He was quick with the weeds. One of the few benefits about him. Honey laid in the corner of the patch the whole time, the shade of the trees doing their best to cool her off. Her heavy husky fur needed to be brushed again. There were tufts sticking out.

"Do you need help with the baking?" He asked while bending down to rub the dirt off his jeans.

"No." I turned around and whistled for Honey.

I didn't miss the frown Elon gave me.

The tarts took most of the night to make. After putting them away so that Honey wouldn't find them, I took to my room to get ready for bed. Mom came in to give her usual goodnight.

"You ready for tomorrow?" she asked. My grandparents only came around once a year or so. They were still bitter over my Mom and her former relationship with my father.

My parents met in college and despite my father's red string connecting to another woman, mom decided she wanted a little piece of him. So she went and fell in love and went against our code. It was when my Dad proposed that my Mom realized she let it go too far. Interfering with the string and fate is a big no-no. So she broke it off and a month later she found out she was pregnant with me. Before I was born she finally pulled the string and made my father get over his heartbreak and look at his future wife. I have never met my father and he doesn't know that I exist.

My grandparents haven't really forgiven my mother for breaking the rule, but they didn't blame me. Mom is convinced they show up to see me. I think they come to see her too just a little bit; they just hide it from her. I can see how their hearts still glow for her.

"Are you?" I retorted back.

Mom sighed before saying, "As ready as I'll ever be." She then turned around and called goodnight over her shoulder.

I did feel bad for my mom. She has never been able to really move on from him. Or maybe she's just afraid of breaking the rules again and keeps herself closed off from any sort of relationship. Maybe it is a self-inflicted punishment. Nonetheless, I wanted her happy.

Patting my bed, beckoning Honey on, I turned off my lamp and shrugged the covers up to my neck. I set my glasses on my night stand and snuggled into my pillow.

*****

My grandparents arrived late into the afternoon. I gave them both a hug in the doorway and then took their coats.

"Mom's setting up for dinner. The Moretti's are here already if you want to go say hi," I said as I hung their jackets in the closet.

"Thanks dear. The living room?"

"Yes, Grandma."

Elon and his family arrived earlier and his mom went straight into the kitchen to help my mom cook the roast. Elon's ten years old little sister had asked to use my laptop and she's been in my room since then. Elon and his father immediately retreated into the living room to watch the football game that should be ending soon.

Elon played football back in middle school, though I knew he did it only for his father. His father played college football before becoming the high school's coach, and on the side played the part of a cupid. I think he enjoyed it well enough, from what I could remember. But I knew it wasn't his passion. When he stopped in ninth grade, his dad understood. We all knew that he liked cooking. Which is good that his parents weren't the controlling type. Really good actually, because this boy could really cook and he brought the goods today. He made this time some kind of potato casserole, mixed grilled veggies, and stuffing that smelled faintly like apples. I'll admit that my mouth started watering the minute they walked in. If there was one good thing about Elon, it was his cooking. Not that I'd ever tell him that.

Honestly? We grew up together and because of that I know a lot about him. Probably more than his actual friends.

And right now? I'm hardcore ignoring the feeling in my stomach at remembering the charming boyish smile he gave me when he first stepped through the door. I didn't have time to think about boys. I had a lot to do to prepare myself for New York.

I walked past the living room and peeked in to see my grandparents sitting on the love seat that sat in the corner of the room. My grandpa was already entranced by the game and my grandma crossed her legs and sat with her hands folded in front of her. It looked like she was patiently waiting for something. Probably dinner.

I walked into the dining room and saw mom and Jannie, Elon's mother, laying down plates on top of cloth placemats.

"The grandparents are here," I announced.

Mom only paused for a second before setting down the last plate and picking up our thick olive colored napkins and started folding them intricately.

"Thank you. Can you go grab some silverware?" She didn't look up. She focused on her origami napkins. I nodded even though, as I realized a second later, she wouldn't see it.

The kitchen was connected to the dining room by a swinging door. I opened a drawer to start collecting forks, spoons, and knives when I heard the door swing open. I turned my head to see Elon. I rolled my eyes and resumed counting the silverware.

"Can we talk?" he asked.

"About what?" I huffed.

He came up next me and rested a hip against the counter.

"Listen, I know we don't get along. Or rather you don't get along with anyone at all."

"For the record, I get along with my dog and my family, and I guess your family too," I grumbled. It seemed like I could get along with everyone decently, except for you it seems.

"Okay, but just listen," he chuckled before getting serious again. "You know my cousin, Len? He bought a building on a corner in New York City. There's room for shops and one of them is a former restaurant. He's asked if I wanted the restaurant. And I really do. I really, really do."

There's another plus side to being cupids. We take our jobs seriously. So that means we help each other find ways to help bring more people together. Even if that means buying a restaurant for your younger cousin.

It was a great opportunity. He's been taking cooking classes and goes to night classes for culinary and business at the local community college. I think he'd be ready for it. He's only been training for nearly four years.

"What does this have to do with me?"

"Well, I need a pastry chef-"

"No."

"Wait! Please just think about it."

I cocked my head to the side and gave him a thoughtful look, before leveling my head and saying no again. I turned and started heading to the dining room.

Elon jumped in front of me. "Please! You make the best desserts. The best ever and I need you. Please give it some more thought. You're relocating to New York anyways aren't you?"

I glared at him. "Why can't you take a no?"

I shoved around him and he called out behind me, "Just wait, Anniel. I'm going to get to you."

Ha. That's what he thinks.

*****

Dinner was uneventful. My grandparents spoke only short pleasantries and Elon's parents took up most of the conversation. I sat quiet for most of it. Only speaking when my grandparents were asking about my grades, how many people I've hooked up, etc.

When my grandparents decided it was time to leave, I went to grab their coats for them.

"Dear, we talked to the headquarters for the New York internet branch. It looks like you'll get in," my grandmother said, taking her coat from my hand.

I smiled wide at her. "Thank you!"

Finally! I felt like I was getting somewhere. For teens or new graduates you had to get an elder cupid's recommendation. Which is where my grandparents came in. They were kind of famous in our world. They were known as the double daters. They put together more couples united than they did when they were apart.

Which kind of makes them the perfect people to give recommendations. I was certain I was a shoe in for the company.

Giving them both a hug goodbye, I closed the door behind them and turned around to see Elon leaning against the wall with his hands in his pockets.

"So you're more than likely moving to the city then? It's kind of perfect, don't you think? You could be working for the internet branch and be sending the couples to my restaurant. And on the side-"

I cut him off. "Why can't you just leave me alone?"

He just stared at me for a few seconds before he started to walk towards me. I tensed up, until he went around me. I turned around to see him grabbing his shoes. He didn't look at me as he slid them on and opened the closet to grab his coat. After shrugging it on, only then did he finally look at me.

"I need you," he said and I could start to feel my heart thump.

"There are millions of other bakers out there. Go find one."

"I don't trust anyone else."

I scrunched up my face. Trust? Seriously? I was terrible to him.

He gave a little laugh. "Yes, you're a little rough around the edges. But I pay attention. I see how you are when you set people up. I know your hidden kindness, your loyalty, your sense of responsibilities. I want you. I need you." And with that he opened the door and left.

I raised my hand to my chest, which was thudding more and more. I knew what was happening. I was a cupid. But that didn't mean I couldn't try to deny it, try to fight it off. But it was getting harder.

Pushing my glasses farther up, I groaned as I headed to my room.

*****

At school the next day I found out that we had a transfer student. From what I could find out his name was Nate and he came from Chicago. He was already wildly popular. There were girls crowding him and yet his string was down.

Every person had a red string that circled their wrist. They couldn't see it of course, only cupids could. When their soul mate wasn't near them their strings floated up towards the sky, but would fade into a faint pink before reaching the ceiling.

This Nate's string was floating to another girl. I believed her name was Casey. She was bookish and quiet. Their romance would be one for the books. Popular new guy and silent smart girl? I nearly smiled at that.

Walking past Casey I started to tap her string lightly. I was caressing it gently before pulling my hand up to tap it some more as I walked down the hallway, towards Nate. I looked up at him to see him staring at Casey. Turning my head, I could see her staring too.

Giving it one last gentle touch, I turned the corner and walked right into someone.

"Oh, sor- never mind," I said as I walked around Elon.

"I seen that," he said as he came up beside me.

"Seen what?"

"You. You were smiling. You do like people. So I wonder if it's only me that you don't like."

I didn't answer.

"Or could it be that you actually like me? Maybe more than you anticipated?"

I stopped in my tracks. I turned to tell him the exact opposite, but he turned around and started walking backwards.

He held out his arms. "And that's perfectly alright. I don't blame you. But don't let your feelings, regardless of what they are, for me stop you from being the best damn baker in New York."

He turned around and walked off whistling. I was bristling with embarrassment and fury. How dare he call me out in front of everyone! But as I looked around I realized no one was staring at me. They were all too wrapped up in themselves.

I sighed and straightened my shoulders. I had to get to Chemistry. The irony wasn't lost on me.

*****

I was pulling weeds out of my garden when I heard Honey give a happy yip. Looking up I saw Elon walking up.

I refrained from shaking my head and went back to work. I didn't say anything either when he started working on the melons. We worked in silence for a while. Then he finally said something.

"I'm graduating early," said Elon.

"Good for you," I replied.

He gave a quiet, little huff. "That means I'm leaving."

I froze. Finally looking up at him I said, "What?"

"My cousin will have the restaurant ready for me in January. He's in the process of buying it now and said that I'll be welcome to come and renovate it then."

But... didn't he want me to bake for him? Was he taking back his invitation?

He must have realized what my shocked and confused expression meant because he said, "That doesn't change a thing. The way I see it my restaurant won't be ready till July. So you still have time to decide if you want to join in. I won't have desserts on the menu unless you're there."

"But you can't just leave off desserts!"

"Well then I guess you'll just have to say yes, then." He stood and wiped off his hands on his jeans before walking away.

I sat there with my mouth hanging open. He was leaving. In a few short months. Then I wouldn't see him at all. My chest was constricting and caving in. I reached up with a dirty hand to find a tear rolling down my cheek. My breath was shuddering and I couldn't help but feel a sob coming up. Standing up I started on my way back home. Honey kept banging her wet nose into my hand. I barely noticed the dirt that was starting to cover her snout.

It wasn't until I was in bed later that night, all clean, did I realize that I had left my basket and all the pulled weeds in the garden. I found that I didn't care.

Three Months Later

He was gone. He left yesterday on a plane straight to New York. He left me a letter that only threatened to not have dessert on his menu. I couldn't help but laugh. He could have texted me his threat.

I didn't want to admit it though, but baking professionally sounded really fun. And hard work too, but nothing I wouldn't be able to handle.

But then again, working in a restaurant was never a part of my plans.

But I would be closer to Elon working in the restaurant.

I wondered what he named it.

Seven Months Later

I've been in New York for a month now. The busy roads, all the street vendors, and all the stores excited me. But I haven't had the heart to find where or even actually go to Elon's restaurant is. I didn't know if I would ever have the courage to.

My work with the internet branch was better than I could have imagined. I'm working on a social media app that deals mostly in pictures. I help couples find each other by the friend suggestions bar that they have.

We wear these special glasses that help calculate their strings. It was amazing to see.

While I haven't visited Elon's restaurant, I have had the courage to look up his website. With the pictures that were featured, I could tell that it was a nice place. Low dim lighting. High tables with nice, tall bar stool like chairs lined the walls while shorter tables and chairs filled up the center of the floor.

He named it 'The Honey Pot'. If I didn't know better I would have thought that he named it after the cartoon bear that he was obsessed with as a child. But it warmed my heart that he named it after my dog. Then again maybe he couldn't think of something original.

I had been sneaking in advertisements onto people's social medias for his restaurant. I couldn't help it. I wanted him to succeed too.

One Month Later

The fool really didn't have a dessert menu.

I was sitting in one of the tall tables in the back corner of the restaurant. I had my head propped up in my hand as I scowled at the menu.

"Have you decided on anything yet, miss?" asked a perky blonde waitress.

"Why isn't there dessert?" I snapped.

Did he want to fail?! He must want to fail. I was going to slap him.

"Sorry, miss. There hasn't been dessert since day one."

"Unbelievable! Where's the owner?"

"He's not here."

I shook my head. "Well go call him and tell him to come here."

The waitress gave me a weird look before walking off. I could see her go up to another, a more plump, brunette, employee. The manager, as the name tag pointed out.

The manager looked at me then nodded to my waitress.

It was a good five minutes before the waitress came back.

"The owner will be here shortly. Shall I get you something to drink in the meantime?" she asked.

"Water, please."

I sat back against my chair. I can't believe it took me this long to get here. Now that I'm here, I felt as if I should have been here ages ago. That I shouldn't have let my fear stop me.

I guess I was just afraid to focus on anything other than being a cupid. I had been my whole life. But did I really think that branching out a little from my original plans would create a disaster?

Lord, if only I wasn't so stubborn and stupid.

Fifteen minutes later, I was swirling my finger along the rim of the glass when I heard him.

"I knew it would be you," Elon said, a bit breathless.

His voice, his appearance, his grin did things to my heart. I think I missed that feeling. Actually I know I did.

"You don't have dessert," I all but growled at him.

"Told you I wouldn't, unless you were here with me."

I sat and stared at him. Finally I said, "I have a few conditions."

His eyes lit up. Actually lit up. He slid into the chair across from me.

"Name it."

"I control the dessert side of the restaurant. I hire and fire bakers. I control all profits made."

"I expected no less. Deal. Let's throw an actual bakery into that deal too."

"Huh?"

"I was thinking that it would be nice for customers to have some desserts to take home. Or if they want to come in just for some, say cookies, they could just come up to that counter that I already have made and buy from there." He was pointing with his thumb over his shoulder. There was a counter with a display case large enough to fit all sorts of treats in there. I did notice it when I first walked in and had wondered about it.

"Deal."

He stuck out his hand and I shook it.

"There's something else," I said. I decided to throw all caution to the wind. Who cared if it made it awkward? I had to try right?

"You were right, all those months ago. I really do like you. Like really, really like you."

He grinned. "Awe, look here folks! I believe she did just say that she's in love with me."

"I didn't say love! I said-"

"That's okay. I like you too."

I smiled. That turned out better than I thought.

"How about lunch tomorrow?" he asked.

I stuck my hand out this time. "Deal!"

Secret Love

By Terri Elders

"You're 15, right babe? So you can catch grunion without a fishing license?"

After all these years I still remember how I whirled around from my open locker, my ponytail nearly smacking Eddie McDaniels' chin. His sea-green eyes searched my face, as if he'd find my birth date inscribed right there on my forehead or cheeks.

"Right?" he asked again.

"Yes, I'm 15. So?"

He flashed me a crooked grin.

I closed the locker door. "Julie's waiting for me," I said, edging down the hall towards the exit.

Eddie fell in beside me. "Uh," he began, "Would you come with me to the Dude's beach party at Tin Can Beach this Saturday? It's a grunion run. We'll roast hot dogs and marshmallows."

I stopped and peered up at him. Was he asking me out on a date? Those ocean eyes, that sun-bleached flattop…I could nearly smell the salt air.

I hoped he wouldn't notice how I'd turned tomato red. Every time I heard Doris Day sing "Secret Love" on the radio, I daydreamed that Eddie would turn out to be more than just my neighbor. We lived on the same block but in radically separate worlds. I was a 'socialite'; he was a surfer. Nonetheless, we had a kind of arrangement. I helped with his homework; he protected me from neighborhood bullies. I idolized him. I kept it a secret, though. You wouldn't catch me shouting about my love from the highest hill or telling any golden daffodils. I was nowhere near as brave as Doris Day.

Once one of our English teachers questioned whether Eddie really had written the report he turned in on Steinbeck's 'The Pearl'. She called him a lounge lizard and glowered at me. I met her gaze without flinching, but after school I hurried to a dictionary. Lounge lizards sponged off women. I wanted to tell

Miss Schmidt that Eddie was no sponger. Because it involved the sea, he had loved that book. He wrote his paper straight from his heart. I just edited it a bit.

My friends had another disparaging name for Eddie...beach bum. While Eddie didn't particularly shine at school, he positively shimmered at the shore. He didn't fall into any other category. He wasn't a motorcycle outlaw, a hood or a Beatnik...he simply surfed. In my eyes he was a surfer king.

"Well?" Eddie asked, shifting from foot to foot in a kind of rangy lopsided shuffle.

"It's a real run, right? No snipe hunts or submarine races?"

Eddie laughed. "Word. The grunion will make the scene. If you're under 16, you don't need a license. The rangers show up, we'll say the batch belongs to you, that you caught them all. It'll be cool."

I stared up at him as I thought it through. Tin Can Beach had a dubious reputation. It derived its name from rusted cans whose lids menaced the bare feet of unwary sunbathers. Nonetheless, vacationing families could pitch a tent, build a bonfire, and camp out there for free. I'd heard that during the Depression people down on their luck even lived there all summer.

I'd never visited the place, just had driven by with my family on the way to visit the Fun Zone at Balboa. My "socialite" friends, the kids who made honor roll, played in the band, produced the school paper, favored Hermosa Beach, where all summer we'd slather ourselves with cocoa butter, body surf and parade up and down the boardwalk sipping Orange Julius shakes. A year earlier two of my girlfriends had tried to teach me to smoke in the women's bathroom. That was about as daring as anybody got at Hermosa.

In those mid-'50s days the serious surfers would hang ten at San Onofre or Malibu. Tin Can Beach drew a different crowd...the guys who swilled beer, siphoned gas, and made out with girls at the passion pit drive-ins. Guys like the Dudes. And like Eddie. Eddie didn't talk much about the Dudes or surfing when we did homework together, but I'd heard the rumors. He was considered a bit rough, a bit rowdy.

But a grunion run! Since childhood I'd read of this uniquely Southern California phenomena, the slippery sardine-like silversides that swarmed ashore at high tide to lay their eggs and spawn. Few of my crowd had seen a run; fewer still had been agile enough to capture any of the tiny fish. Even if I were there only as a lookout for rangers, I'd still be with Eddie. And I'd have been to a grunion run, a landmark event.

"All right, Eddie. Just promise... no beer. My dad would have kittens!"

"Crazy, babe. Later!" Eddie sprinted back up the corridor and I exited towards the quad. I could hardly wait to tell Julie.

*****

"Eddie McDaniels? You're loco," Julie said, rolling her eyes, just as I knew she would.

"Hey," I countered, "If we actually catch any grunion, I'll have a topic for my science report!"

Julie shook her head. "Just be careful," she cautioned, "The Dudes are pretty wild."

"I trust Eddie," I said, remembering how he'd stood up for me years before when the kids who'd congregated on our corner had thrown spitballs at me when I'd roller-skated by.

*****

That Saturday I dressed carefully in jeans, a pink pullover sweater and saddle shoes. I took extra care tying back my ponytail with a pink grosgrain ribbon, and applied a little mascara and Pink Queen lipstick. I even splashed some Aprodisia cologne behind my ears and on my wrists.

Despite the balmy spring air, I knew that even summer nights could turn chilly at the beach. I borrowed Dad's black leather jacket, promising to take good care of it.

"You look pretty cool, babe," Eddie said when he picked me up. I ducked my head so he wouldn't see me blush. The last thing I wanted him to know was how much his casual compliment meant to me.

By sundown the Dudes had a bonfire snapping and crackling. I threaded a pair of wieners on a straightened out wire coat hanger and started to roast them. Eddie declined an offer of a beer, and fished a couple of bottles of Coke out of an ice-filled washtub.

"Hey, Eddie, what's up with the Coke? Is your date a wet blanket?" A couple of the Dudes frowned in my direction. I held my breath. I didn't want to hear Eddie denying that I was his date or explaining that he'd only dragged me along to act as a decoy.

Eddie ignored them though, and just walked over and handed me a Coke. "Hey, babe," he whispered, "Don't get frosted at those guys. Sometimes they go ape at the beach. They don't know no better." He sat down beside me on an old Army blanket he'd taken from the trunk of his old Chevy. My hot dog tasted pretty good, even without the mustard, which I'd skipped to avoid dripping anything on Dad's jacket.

Under the radiant full moon it was easy to pick out the couples now cocooned in their blankets. From time to time I could hear a pop as another beer can lid was skewered by the punchers the guys called church keys. But Eddie and I just sat quietly, eating our hot dogs and gazing out at the sea, waiting to greet the fish. We had our flashlights and gunny sacks ready.

Soon we heard a shout from down the beach, and then the shoreline lit up as everybody rushed forward, waving flashlights. We bolted for the water. As the fish-filled waves broke, Eddie dug at the sand, snatching up handfuls of grunion while I held open the bag.

Suddenly one of the Dudes drew near. "Hey, Eddie," he yelled, "Gonna be a killjoy all night long?" He waved a beer can around wildly, flicking foam towards us. I backed away, terrified of staining Dad's jacket.

Eddie stood his ground, motioning me back towards the fire. I watched him wait for the next wave, then tackle the menacing Dude just before it broke. He laughed as froth from the overturned beer mated with froth from the waves.

"Come on, babe," he said. "Let's cut out. I'll take you home. You don't have to lie to the rangers for those jerks. Good thing no beer got on that jacket!"

When we got to my house Eddie offered to walk me to the door, but I declined. I wanted to avoid any awkward goodnights on my porch. I didn't want Eddie to think he was obligated to give me a hug…or even more embarrassing, a kiss.

"It's ok. The porch light is on, and my folks are still up." I hopped out of the Chevy and started up the walk.

*****

I saw Julie on Monday morning. "Well?"

"The Dudes were wild, but Eddie protected me. He always has. So I guess I'll help him write his science paper on the grunion, instead of writing my own about them." Julie just laughed.

*****

I didn't see much of Eddie that summer and when school started he didn't show up. I learned from his brother that he had gone to live in Hawaii with some cousins. He'd finish his senior year in Honolulu. Years later on a cable television show I saw him again. He was as bronzed, sun-bleached, and ocean-eyed as ever and he'd just won a surfing trophy. Still chasing a wave.

Not long ago at a high school reunion, I ran into that menacing Dude from the grunion run. "Yeah, I remember you. You were the wet blanket that time when that big Kahuna, Eddie McDaniels, dunked me in the surf," he said.

"That was me," I agreed. "But, man," I continued, "the wet blanket I remember most was the one you wrapped yourself up in after you took that unexpected tumble into the surf." I smirked, just as if I were fifteen again.

Secret loves aren't secret if anybody ever knows. I'd never told a soul about my love for Eddie, not even Julie. A few minutes after I'd bantered with the Dude, Eddie McDaniels walked into the party. Though his hair had turned completely silver, he still looked tan and fit. I held my breath as he approached me.

He just stood there, staring at me. Finally he nodded. "Babe," he said, "When we were kids you had a crush on me and I knew it. I was going to tell you how much I cared for you the night I took you to the grunion run. I was going to ask you if you'd wait for me until we both grew up a little. But I was a chicken, when you jumped out of my car, I should have run after you. I've always regretted that I didn't."

Once again I turned tomato-red. This time I didn't duck my head, but I stifled a sob as Eddie McDaniels, after five decades finally took me in his arms and kissed me. It was worth waiting for. He held me tight until my husband walked up and asked to be introduced.

I winked at my husband. He winked back. He understood about love and kisses…and memories.

Defining Me

By Melissa Meeks

Only the One who created me
Can define who I am
Choices influence feeling and circumstances
But will never change Your love for me

I am Your Beloved,
A princess, daughter of the King
Your truth cannot change
You remain the same for eternity

I am unique, designed for a special role
Conceived by my heavenly Father's vast imagination
There are no auditions
You embossed the script on my heart

If I define myself apart from Your design
The mire of life encompasses me
Your map for my journey becomes illegible
The path fades to nothingness

When I turn back to Your open arms
The way is obvious once more
Pursuing Your intent for me elicits true fulfillment
Your delight in me flourishes.

Full Moon over Apple Valley

By Mary Langer Thompson

We argue about whether it is full
or not.
I say yes,
you say no, because you see
the edge, the margin
outlined with small shadows.
I believe the night will clarify it.

I'd like to pluck it down into my hands,
show you because it's so far away, you can't tell.
Trust me, Golden Delicious of my Apple Valley eye,
the moon is full tonight.

END OF ISLAND LIFE
By Rhonda Wiley Jones

Last year's trip to Isla Mujeres proved a repeat of years before, carefree; but not this time.

Clara, always the light in Ben's world, carried dark lines under her eyes. She walked at the pace of a turtle. They had sold their landscape business to retire two years ago. Breast cancer arrived a year and a half later. Determined, she intended to make one last visit to their island to say good-bye to friends and make lasting memories for Ben.

Arriving in Cancun en route to the island, an airline representative wheeled Clara, from plane to immigration to baggage claim and through customs. Ben followed carting their luggage. She stewed each stretch of the way about 'the fuss' being made over her.

Curbside, Ben confirmed transit to the ferry. Now out of the wheel chair Clara leaned against a concrete pillar, wiping her forehead and neck. Limo personnel placed her in the air-conditioned van, then their luggage. Ben offered her lukewarm bottled water. She sipped, made a face, and handed it back.

Once at the ferry dock in Cancun, he made arrangements with a maletero who loaded their baggage on a dolly and offered a wheelchair for her. He stayed with Ben and Clara until it was time to board. At the footbridge, she walked across, Ben in front guiding her and the maletero supporting her from behind. She collapsed into an aisle seat and relished the clear, aqua Caribbean water out the window lapping against the boat like always.

Ben sat across the aisle from her. She turned to him and said, "Will you come back without me next year? I hope you will."

"I am not thinking that far ahead. I just want to enjoy this year with you." He reached across the aisle and squeezed her hand.

She returned the embrace of his hand, then gazed back out to the channel water kissing the sides of the boat and said, "This is what I want heaven to look like."

She managed that sly smile that had set his heart on fire so many years ago, and today shattered it. She could always tease him with a smile or a cock of her head. He had learned to read the intent of each, which she used to her advantage. Humor was her golden touch, but today Ben ached with each encounter. "Let's not talk about it." He buried his head in tickets and reservation numbers, wishing to avoid her question.

She said, "Remember the first year we scorched ourselves on the beach?" He nodded to her and she continued, "And the next year when they planted all those tiny palm trees? We each sat with our back against a scrawny stalk that gave the barest of shade and no breeze."

He gave in and offered his attention. "Yes," he chuckled, "and scorched again that year."

Clara leaned her head back and closed her eyes. She wanted this trip to be happy for Ben, for him to be able to forget. She had already broken that promise to herself.

Ben noted her pale, thin skin. He knew to shield her from the sun this year; and knew that she would resist.

When the ferry docked on the island, local business people and eager tourists surged off the boat. Ben and Clara waited for the ferry to empty; but feared others would take the maletero, Luis, who typically escorted them. Nevertheless, he had waited knowing their arrival date from friends already on the island. He usually carted their luggage to the apartment as they walked alongside and chatted. This time he hailed a taxi at Ben's request.

When they reached their island apartment, Clara started to unpack and arrange things like always.

Ben said, "Why don't you lie down for a while and rest?"

"But the apartment won't be livable until we settle in." Her friends had cautioned Ben about Clara not getting enough rest, because they knew her full-throttle nature. Their insinuations infuriated him that he did not know how to care for her.

She finally agreed to a short nap.

He set about unpacking what he could without keeping her awake. After a while, he went down the street to order lime sopa at Antonio's Café and have it waiting for her supper.

Antonio was not there, but he left a message with the English-speaking cook to inform Antonio that Clara was frail and ill. She had always looked younger than she was the mark of health and vibrancy. Antonio had often joked with Ben about his youthful wife.

Once awake and aware of the savory scent of soup, Clara's recall was stronger than her voice. Standing in the doorway she said, "The first time we stepped foot in Antonio's, he greeted us like we were the only customers, though it was packed." She enjoyed the favored attentiveness Antonio always provided. Clara crooned, "Charming fellow that Antonio! I missed seeing him this afternoon. You should have waited until I was up."

"I wanted to have it waiting for you." That seemed to appease her.

"Remember, we went early the first night to his place because we had such an appetite after sunning, swimming, and…," Clara lowered her voice, as if someone might hear her, "making love. We were ravenous." That same cunning smile slipped out and her chemo-drugged eyes twinkled. "Do you remember?"

Ben whispered to her, "Sure I do; couldn't forget it." The single dimple on his left cheek deepened as his gray eyes searched hers.

Ben knew he was a lucky man; she was such a tease. When they were younger, Clara could startle him, jumping out from the laundry room when he arrived home. On the other hand, she would inform him of their next date night location; from the kids' bowling alley for greasy hot dogs, to the Chez Francesca for a four-star dinner date. She never let a chance pass to razz him about how much she spent on clothes, which he never understood. Moreover, she never hid things from him like so many women, but found reasons to make fun of everything.

She reached up to touch the dimple and cupped his face in her hand. He leaned down to grant her wish—a kiss. The sands of time, slipping through their fingers, had brought a newfound thoughtfulness and tenderness; they had forgotten sometimes through the years.

Sitting down, Clara spooned the soup, working her way around the slices of lime. Ben reached across his plate of pulled pork and forked out the limes one at a time.

"Gracias, mi amor," Clara said with a weak voice.

"De nada."

She ate only three or four more bites. The bowl sat in front of her—half-empty in her eyes; half-full in his.

The following morning, Clara woke early to make coffee. She used to perk it every morning, but recently, she had not had the strength.

He found her in the kitchenette fumbling with the grounds. When he walked in and said quietly, "I caught you," she jumped and spilled them. They laughed over the mess and fell into each other's arms.

"I'll clean that up and finish making coffee." He got a damp cloth to pick up the grounds.

Clara said, "After coffee, I want to visit Katrina and pick up some veggies from Ida."

"You have the stamina for all that?"

"Maybe. We'll see."

He and Clara relished their cups of coffee together this morning, one of their long-held traditions as a couple. He had taught her how to enjoy coffee early in the marriage, and through the years and even after the arrival of the kids, they always carved out time to share at least one cup.

Later they moseyed over to Katrina's house, wedged between two storefronts. Clara had emailed ahead to forewarn her of what to expect.

Ben knocked, and moved to the tiny window to wave at Sofia, the four-year-old princess. As her mother opened the door, she squealed, ran past Clara, and flung her arms around Ben's legs. Last year, he had brought the princess ice cream every day while she recovered from a tonsillectomy. She remembered the words in English.

"Ice cream? Ice cream?"

"Not today, sweetie." She understood the shake of his head, not his words.

They entered the tight confines of the house. As if she had been there yesterday, Clara sat down at the kitchen table with

Katrina, a native to the island and a nurse educated in the United States. Ben carried Sofia across the tiny living room, hanging on his leg and plopped into a chair. Ben played with Sophia so Clara could use her energy to exchange months of gossip. Because Clara had reveled in the street shenanigans of a motorcyclist last year, Katrina told her the latest. The young man who had laid his Harley down in the street to confront another tourist had tried it again with a different outcome this year. Katrina said, "The authorities told him, 'Jail tonight, and an escort to the ferry tomorrow morning. You are not welcomed back.'"

Ben and Clara laughed at how differently the Mexican legal system worked compared to their own.

Katrina complained that drugs continued to snake their way onto the island. "So far the dealings are meager. Thankfully, drug lords need more dolores to be interested."

Clara had always enjoyed gossip; juicy tidbits whether funny, adventurous, or exciting. Never did she delight in the true injustices of life; but an example of irony tempted her greatly.

Changing the subject, Katrina said, "And the dogs are multiplying like rabbits. Dr. Valentino continues to offer spay and neutering clinics. But the men on the island insist the dogs need their male parts."

Clara quipped lightly, "Valentino should neuter some of the men, I suspect. These poor women carry babies half their lives."

Katrina nodded agreement. The nurse in her wanted to know, "How has your year been? Chemo isn't easy."

Clara chuckled. "I'm a mere shadow of myself. Oh, what I would have given for that once upon a time." Then she sobered. "But it's been tough on Ben, too," she said as she shifted her gaze to him. "He's been the best nurse. Cook, too. He's been with me every step of the way."

"Not a very good nurse," he said.

Katrina, understanding the role, said, "I know it is not a job all of us would take on by choice, but I know you, Ben. Loving and helpful."

"You're too kind, Katrina. All those people always calling to ask about her, I just wanted to yell, 'it's none of your business'. But she insists I answer all those calls and be nice about it." He blinked, locked eyes with Clara, and smiled as if to say, 'I understand'.

Turning back to Katrina, Clara said, "Surgery was a cake walk, compared to chemo; wished I could have died some days."

"Now, Clara, don't talk that way," Ben said.

"I know, but she gets it."

Katrina nodded and explained she had to make dinner before she left for her shift. Clara, always one to honor other people's needs, knew that Katrina had sensed her exhaustion.

Clara returned to bed regretfully without visiting Ida, the vegetable woman. Ben promised to shop for veggies and groceries. "Yes, I'll be sure to get the ingredients to make Mexican hot chocolate. ... Yep, I know which brand."

When he returned from the store, Ben put the groceries away. The dishes, used by the last renters, were not always clean, so each year Clara washed and put them away sparkling. This year Ben prepared the kitchen, as she liked it, though he would be the one to use it. *If I'm back next year, I can set it up my way.* He worked in slow motion, reminiscing about her contentment in prior years with getting the place 'in shape'.

As he waited for her to rally, he reached for last week's issue of Time magazine. After a while, she warmed his shoulder with a firm touch. He recognized the pressure of her hands, that she needed something and said, "What can I do for you, my darling?"

He turned to see apprehension in her eyes.

"I need my meds. You packed."

"Yes, I'll get them. You sit."

He went straight for her pills and a glass of water. "You want a bite to eat with these, a peanut butter sandwich? I can make it." He watched her fretfulness as she swallowed the pills and shook her head.

"No? Well, how about some cocoa?"

She refused speechlessly again, and then said, "Tonight, we need to see Antonio. He's expecting us."

She paced the floor, a sweater pulled tight around her. When the pills arrived too late to forestall the pain, she would walk it through. She took the pills at prescribed times, but sleep did not always match pill time. She paced until the pain subsided and returned to bed.

Up again that evening, Clara slowly searched for a change of clothes. Always a clotheshorse, she had brought things that no longer fit; she had lost too many pounds. Her friends at home would be appalled at her lack of interest in clothes. And shoes? She brought only four pairs, not the usual eight.

Antonio was sweeping the front steps when they arrived. He had set tables and prepared the grill. He looked up when he heard Ben's voice. "Antonio, mi amigo. Que tal?"

"Muy bien! E tu?"

Antonio encircled Ben's lean form heartily with both arms, as Clara looked on, smiling.

"And me, what about me?" she asked with willowy arms outstretched.

Antonio stepped down to street level and gently kissed Clara's hollow cheek, noticing the parchment-like skin. The reedy forearms in his hands lacked muscle. He stepped back and helped her gingerly up the two steps to the nearest table, their table.

"Tonight, the best grouper to be grilled in tin foil, just as you like it. Margaritas?" He needed only their smiles to leave and mix their drinks.

Ben said, "Of course," to his back.

When he served the margaritas, he leaned over to Clara. "Mi amiga, you are not well. What is wrong?"

When she hesitated, Antonio knelt beside her and asked, "You have come to say good-bye?" She nodded with sad eyes; then tried on her fake pouting smile. Ben watched and ached knowing what the exchange between the two friends meant.

Antonio continued in earnest, "To say good-bye is only temporary. In time, we will see each other again, I know."

His demeanor shifted. "But tonight, we celebrate."

Clara raised her hands to a setting sun and danced in her seat. "Yes, we will celebrate that annoying rooster of yours." Her playful scowl turned to a smile. "Also the sun's warmth, the palm trees' shade, the ocean's breeze." She swayed to soundless music, "We will move to la música."

This was the Clara Ben had known all these years—the one who made the most of every day. This moment would burn a place in his heart; one he would recall when she was gone.

Early to bed gave Clara the rest she needed to join the rooster the next morning. She made coffee for Ben again with a certain pride in her ability to do something for him.

Ben entered, appearing tired. "You look lovely this morning, my beauty," he said.

"Oh, you always say that." She handed him a cup of coffee. "The sun and sea are calling. Let's go to the beach today."

"Okay, let's do it. I'll help you get dressed." Ben, concerned it would take too much, knew this was exactly why they had come. His fretting over her sapped his energy, but if she could take to the beach, so could he.

The taxi driver dropped them off at the two-story-high, yellow blow-up bottle of Corona, next to Buho's bar. Clara kicked off her sandals and headed for the water's edge.

Tomaso, the umbrella vendor, ran to greet them. "Señor Ben, Señora Clara, buenos días. Bienvenidos! Good to see you. I will get chairs and umbrella." He stood a moment looking bewildered, as if trying to discern what could be the matter, but decided to get chairs instead.

Clara noted his hesitancy and said when he returned, "I have been sick this year, but so much better," she raised her face to the sun, "now that the sun is on my face. I'll have my toes in the water soon."

"Bueno."

Ben and Clara settled in. Always a people-watcher, Clara also served as fashion police. She surprised Ben by closing her eyes. He scanned her frail body, which had fit into a two-piece last year. Her gaunt figure now dictated she wear shorts and a tee to hide her fading frame.

She said, "Tell me what's happening on the beach."

"Volleyball. A dog in the water chasing kids. One amateurish sandcastle being built."

"No, you know what I mean. Details, about the women. More thongs displaying lovely buns than usual? Florals or geometrics in swimsuit designs? And yes, how many boob jobs? The important things."

"You mean I have permission to gawk?"

"No-o-o. Just gaze nonchalantly. Scan the beach. Take it all in, in one broad sweep. Don't stare at a single set, Ben," she chided as she opened one eye and lifted that eyebrow at him. "You know better."

"But you know I like specifics. I'm not good at taking in that big picture and capturing the details without zeroing in, focusing. That's what we guys do."

Clara raised her body up on an elbow, opened her eyes, and said, "I see I must survey myself. You are hopeless. Not helpless, just hopeless." They laughed.

"Not much has changed. Maybe more electric colors this year."

He mused whether he could come back without seeing the beach through her eyes.

As she closed her eyes and rested her head again, she said, "More bare breasts too. There must be more Europeans. Do you remember when I went topless, when I still had perky ones?"

"Sure do. I also recall I had to talk you into taking off your top the first time. You thought it was too risqué; but I knew you wanted to."

"Hate to admit it. I did want to. And you did talk me into it. I loved the freedom. You guys are lucky, you know. No shirt, no problem. No bathroom, no problem."

"I like topless," Ben said.

Clara tapped his arm, "You always have."

In days gone by, she would have sucker-punched him and he would have feigned spilling into the sand. But today, all she could do was insinuate. He still pretended to fall.

Ben said, "If I didn't know better—from direct, personal experience—I would think you prefer women to men."

"I just enjoy the study of women. I'm a... contemporary anthropologist."

I'll always see the beach through her eyes. "Oh that's it, is it?" Ben stroked her leg. I'll miss these moments.

Pedro, a jewelry peddler and her friend, stopped to remind them as he always had, "El sol es bueno." He took in her sunken eyes and bony body and said, "Jew'ry for the lady?" He opened his arms wide, laden with necklaces and bracelets dangling for her to inspect. She fingered bracelets that would hang too large on her wrists this year.

"Not today."

"Ah, no hoy?"

Clara smiled weakly and repeated, "Not today."

He moved on.

Clara said, "Ben, you must continue to come back to the island. To see our friends. They will miss you, if you're not back."

"I can't even imagine returning without you, my love. It would never be the same."

"Of course not. But you love this place as much as I do. There is no reason for you to stay home and mope. Pauline is back without Matt this year."

"I'm not Pauline."

"And Janice, she waited two years, but she is back and she seems content to be here again."

"I'm a man, not Janice or Pauline."

"I know; but promise me this: you will visit the island next year or the next and find happiness here again in your own way."

"Clara, I can't make that promise."

"Then just try. Okay?"

He smiled at her without replying.

The skinny palm trees, which had been planted the second year they visited, now towered overhead and offered shade that made the mid-morning heat bearable. The breeze tousled Clara's blond hair, grown out wavy and with a hint of red after chemotherapy.

The day in the shade, visiting with friends, took a toll on her.

On their fourth morning, he crawled out of bed before she did and made coffee. The smell of the brew startled her awake. The delight of a mug served to her in bed replaced the disappointment of oversleeping and not getting to make it for him.

"You beat me to it today."

"I added cinnamon. Do you like it?"

"Yes, the aroma captivates my Mexican sensibilities," she said, as if a gourmand.

Even after a fitful night for Clara, she insisted they return to the beach. She moved more slowly and with less gusto than yesterday while dressing. Ben, too, felt the weight of the days on him, as well. They arrived later than the day before.

Miriam, the Mayan businesswoman who sold wraps, cloth bags, and baskets, would in years past carry her bebes on her back until each child walked. She stopped to visit Clara. "Buenos días, mi amiga. You need el pareó o la bolsa?"

Ben knew Clara wanted nothing today; however, in the past she had always bought items for herself and friends back home. Today, she asked about Miriam's growing children and business through single words and sign language. Puzzled by Clara's gaunt looks, Miriam asked by clutching her heart if Clara's heart was okay. Clara placed her hand on her heart and said, "Bueno." She opened her right hand with her left down and then flipped them, from life to death.

Miriam laid her hands on Clara's arm and said, "Adieu, mi amiga, Dios vaya con usted." She knew this was a final so long. As she walked away, she turned back to throw a kiss to Clara. Clara touched her heart and threw double kisses to Miriam. Tears streaked each face.

Ben watched Clara finalize today's beach survey of women and fashion quickly, then close her eyes. I can't do this next year. After a while, Ben caught her viewing the beach. She said, "I need to feel the sea on my feet. Let's take a short walk."

Ben helped her from the chair and she wrapped a pareó around her shoulders. They stepped into the cool water and it took her breath away. Clara shivered and giggled. As she adjusted to the temperature, she waded in thigh-high.

Ben would never feel the water here without thinking of how much she loved it.

Clara longed to stay, but after a bit, felt wasted. Two years ago, they would have stayed at the beach all day; swum twice; walked the shoreline; and snorkeled on calm, sunny days. They never tired of the repetitive nature of the sea and its amenities. Instead, Ben unaccustomed to seeing her energy fail, took her home early and served her a concoction of pills to ease the pain.

After a long nap, Clara was up and pacing again with a pain that now clung to her insides. The pain emanated from her midsection, but reached the farthest corners of her little toes. She strode the small space of their apartment, fought with the wrapper of chips that she could not open. "Damn packaging."

Ben said, "I know. Here, let me."

Clara pushed it toward him, folded her arms, and stalked to the bathroom to take another pill. She returned to sit with her book and chips. She reread one page four times, then dropped it by her chair. She circled the room aimlessly, looked out the window, rearranged some stacked books. Ben, knowing there was nothing to do, tried to read but could not. The pain slowly subsided, and she went to bed to sleep, deep and long.

The sun lay low in the sky when Clara awakened. She said, "Let's go watch the sun set. Can you make a piña colada?"

"Sure." He was happy to see her rally. Frances, a neighbor back home and confidant of Clara's had told him before they left that Clara would not let this ailment keep her down. But Frances did not know how much it already had taken from her before arriving.

The two crossed the street, took a shortcut through an alleyway, and walked to the malecón wall to sit with their piña coladas. They sipped in silence. She reached for Ben's hand. I can't do this without her next year. He set his glass down, wrapped one arm around her, and offered his other hand.

Ben said, "We used to watch the sun set every evening here."

"Yes, and we would bounce out of bed and hike to the other side for sunrise."

"We saluted the day on either end."

Clara said, "Every day is priceless with you. And the kids."

The kids thought she should go again this year. They, like Frances thought she was up to it, as Clara seemed to. Or did she? Frances and the kids thought it would be a relaxing trip. Clara always presented a confident 'all-is-okay' front to friends and family. But Ben knew better.

He wanted to say what was in his heart, to let her know she could let down her guard with him. He also knew she would rebuff him, if he talked like this.

Unable to speak, Ben hugged her lightly, when he wanted so much to squeeze. His emptiness grew larger as the sun set and withdrew from the horizon, only the glow of day left. He gazed on the sky, trying not to let her see how the anticipated loneliness overtook him.

He asked with an even voice, "What do you want to do tomorrow, hon?"

"I want to see tomorrow."

Tears slipped from his eyes. She laid her head on his shoulder and he pulled her closer to him. Tears slid to his chin and into her hair. He felt her tears on his arm.

That night, back in the apartment as he meted out her medicine, she said, "I wasn't kidding when I said I want to see tomorrow." Maybe this was the time to let her know she could admit her failing body. Then she turned her head sideways and said, "But I also want to snorkel."

"What? You up to it?"

"I'll find out tomorrow." She sounded hopeful at the moment.

The following day they taxied to the beach with snorkel gear. Ben carried it to the entry point on the beach for her. She donned the gear with his help, but slipped and fell several times in her attempts. Eventually Clara floated into the water. She swam out a ways and motioned for him.

Ben came alongside her. She drifted and pointed to a conch shell. He dove for it. She smiled and looked inside when Ben surfaced with it. "Oh, I forget it stinks. Let's leave it."

Ben dropped it back into the sea.

Always at home in the water, Clara gained energy from paddling in fins with little effort. Her enjoyment of the ocean encouraged Ben. The weightlessness felt freeing; Clara however did not last long, she was used to carrying a light and energetic body made for fun, now full of weariness. She fell on the beach, limp with exertion, to dry off herself before returning home. Ben helped.

When they arrived back at the apartment, Clara returned to bed 'for just a short one'. Like the drunks on the island, a 'short one' grew to another long one, and one was not enough. She spent the rest of the day in and out of bed recovering. After making lunch from leftovers, Ben sat on the porch and waited for her to get up.

He worried over whether he had been wise to bring her. The kids knew how much she lived for this time in Mexico each year; but they had no idea what it would take out of her. He had anticipated the strenuous travel would tax her body, willing as she was. He knew navigating the cobblestone streets and the sandy beach would wear her out quickly. He knew the heat and wind would take its toll.

He knew equally that she needed to dance in her chair, to walk the beach, smell the salt-water, taste the fresh catch-of-the-day. But mostly she needed to say good-bye, while he needed lasting memories of one more time on the island with her. *There's no way I'll be back next year.*

Sniffing the cinnamon in the Mexican hot cocoa later that evening, she said, "I'm afraid I don't have the stamina to see everyone, to say all my good-byes."

"We'll do what we can; we've done too much today. You just need another day to rest."

"Yes, tomorrow is another day. Tammi and Floyd. We need to stop by and see them, as well as Gaylene and Herb. You're right. There's plenty of time."

He sat, staring at her hollowed-out cheeks and sagging eyelids. He raised a simple prayer: *Let her see our friends one more time.*

The next morning, Ben made coffee and took a cup to Clara. She refused and turned over with a moan. He took the coffee back to the kitchen and sat thinking about the days when they had played volleyball on the beach with strangers from around the world. When younger, their vivacious bodies had craved the challenge of walking a full circle of the island, a bit over ten miles. They had run a 10K race, not to win, but to raise money for the care of the island dogs. And yes, at the end of sweaty, beach-filled days they would come back to the apartment to clean up, make love, and nap before heading out for dinner and dancing.

Ben reprimanded himself, "Got to stay ahead of the pain. Get the pills in her."

When she took the pills, Clara said quietly, "I don't know how much longer I can hang on." That admission punctured the hope he held onto for her. "I came to say good-bye to friends. But now I'm just trying to make it home to see the kids."

"We will make it home fine to see Mitch and Brandy."

"I know. I'm trying." Somewhere deep in the cancerous and drugged tissue of what was left of her body she knew without knowing how.

Neither of them could cry, only sigh. Ben sat on the edge of the bed holding her hand.

Later, as he slept next to her, Clara twitched and gasped for breath. Ben thought, the doctor told us this could happen.

He woke Clara to give her the cocktail of relief. She fell back to sleep without hesitation. He watched her breathe with a change in the rhythm; the physical changes the doctor had said might begin started to mount. He witnessed each shift in behavior, mood, and bodily function.

The next day Ben walked a half-mile to the island doctor's office. Dr. Saltillo said he would come to their apartment shortly after noon. Relieved, Ben had returned to the apartment and Clara's side of the bed to watch the body he had loved for decades now wasted. Lord, let Clara make it back home to the kids.

Clara later got up, shuffled around the room, talking to herself. He tried to get her back to bed, but she would not go. He offered lunch. She shook her head no, fingered her nightshirt, and paced. The ache he had kept muffled now roared fiercely inside him.

The doctor came that afternoon and told Ben, "She is not up to going home now. You can take her to the hospital on the mainland in Cancun. Or you can keep her here and let her go."

Ben, not ready for the inevitable, knew there was nothing left to do but spend these last days alone on the island, together. No room in his head existed to think of another year, of returning without her.

Ben wandered the two rooms that Clara had just yesterday paced in pain. They had intended to spend lucid, real moments that would reinforce lasting memories of their decades together on the island. Instead, moments of clarity came and went for her.

After the doctor left, Clara said, "Loved you… since the fair. Melissa Watts."

"Oh, I had my eye on you, even with Melissa on my arm. She didn't hold a candle to you," he said playfully. Ben smoothed the hair out of her eyes and smiled at her.

Clara calmed as he hummed "Amazing Grace." She loved the song, sang it reverently around the house or when washing dishes—so unlike her typical sassy self. Today her struggle for breath took away the strength to walk until the medicine took effect. Ben watched while she swatted at phantoms.

Clara made quiet gurgling sounds, as if she had drunk iced tea and had lain down too quickly. He raised her head and shoulders up to let her cough, swallow, and recover. It seemed she did not sense him helping.

He napped until she wrestled and flailed the bed sheets back. Startled, he leaned over and tried to ease her. Clara fussed, until he backed off to let her fight those demons herself.

She settled down and in moments of clarity looked him in the eye and said, "Ben, remember the flute music at Maria Pilar's?"

Ben leaned forward and said, "Yes, you felt it had to be Ecuadorian—didn't know though. It floated up from the bar below and seemed as if it had all the time in the world. The bongos, the easy guitar...."

She said, "Felt like… carrying me out to sea."

Ben teased, "No, that was me, remember? I carried you wave after wave out to sea that night." The twinkle in her eyes was all he needed to know she remembered.

Ben went on, "Another night, a different year, you pointed to the full moon framed by dead tree limbs."

She recollected, "Moon's halo…."

"Yes, the halo was six times its size. We stepped into the street and danced to 'You're Still the One'."

Beaming Clara said, "You are," and then the smile faded. She fingered the sheets again.

Ben went to the kitchen to make supper for himself. He tried to stay awake in his chair, but nodded off. Later he took her to the bathroom, insisted on crackers with her medicine, and crawled into bed with her. In the old days, just weeks and months ago, she would fuss if he had to help her do anything. So self-determined was she that even the kids called her Independent Inez behind her back. He fell asleep, in spite of his intention not to, holding her hand.

In a restless sleep, Ben heard the tide breathing. The air shifted and it seemed as if energy surged all around him. A huge drawing noise filled the space—a negative pull on his entire body. Next, a consuming rush of electricity, motion, and sound engulfed him with the smell of sulfur. Finally, a wall of water directed its path and power toward him. He watched with unfettered fear as the tsunami set him awash in a churning inferno of water. Chairs and tables, doors and dishes, motorcycles and playground equipment swirled through the water, like clothes in a washing machine, only infinite.

The dread he felt matched the intensity of the storming seawater. He heard a gurgling noise, like someone else, not him, drowning. That person's panic fused with his. Time carried no meaning in the torrent, until he landed on something solid.

The storm stranded him on the peak of a hill with a view of retreating water, receding with the same fierceness that it had come. And he saw Clara. He heard the gurgling, gasping noise coming from her limp body, washing out to sea. He bellowed for her. Clara's body floated away from him. He scrambled down the hill; tumbling, clawing his way toward the ocean. He could not hear his own cries to save her.

Clara coughing and gasping for air woke him from the nightmare. She now looked at him wide-eyed and sputtering, like the kids did when they took their first dunk in a pool and came up surprised. He pulled her back down in the bed and stroked her cheek.

His voice cracked. "I can't save you, Clara." Tears tumbled down his face. "I want to, but I can't." He held her tight. "I love you. I always will."

Ben cradled her for some time, sobbing. Exhausted, his tears dried up and he crawled out of bed to sit in a chair by her bed. He tried to nap and could not, then picked up Time magazine and attempted to read.

Clara slept in fits and starts. Wondering if she was conscious, he watched every twitch in her face, every apparition she swiped in space. From time to time, she would cough, as if choking on something she had eaten. Each time she recovered with or without his aid.

And then her eyebrows unfurled and her forehead smoothed.

Ben sat straight up, held his breath, and reached for her hand. It lay ivory-like in his.

Then her jaw loosened and her chin dropped ever so little. Her head fell to the left away from him faintly. And the telltale sign assured him: her lids went limp and those green eyes that had captured him years ago stared into space.

Gently, as if not to wake her, he crawled into bed next to her, laying an arm across her still body.

Memories crashed against one another. Her lovely red hair veiling her face at the end of the aisle. Perspiration streaming from her face as she took Mitch and later Brandy into her arms. Arms covered in dirt as she lugged a shrub to display. Her youthful body striding the beach next to him. Always proud of her; always pleased he had found her.

The doctor thought you had more time. A wave of unbearable, deep emptiness struck and he wept. Tears soaked the bed beneath him.

After the doctor declared her deceased, Ben called Mitch and Brandy. While he spoke with each of them, he broke down. "Your mother passed away early this morning. ... We didn't expect…. I didn't know, but maybe she wanted to die here."

He continued, "The laws in Mexico mean it is easier for me to bring your mother's ashes back. You won't see her body. You'll have to remember her alive. I hope you understand."

They each said, "Of course, Dad."

Two days later, Ben packed Clara's ashes in a bag that she had toted to the beach for more than fifteen years. He carried the precious contents with him to breakfast. There was a table pushed into the corner with two sides of it available, but a large group had taken the second chair. He needed only the one, so he gingerly sat the beach bag down and ordered.

When the group broke up, a man set a chair back at Ben's table and said, "For your lady this morning." The chair sat in its place, pulled out waiting for Clara. The fellow walked away.

Ben sat puzzled by the stranger's words; when he felt a slight breeze, as if Clara's skirt had just whipped about when she sat down to join him.

HEART BREEZE
By Divya Bhavana Didla

Tender love, what a breeze you bought for me.
As a lone star in the sky traveled till now,
You awaken me, as an early morning wind bloom the buds.
Like drizzle, cloudy muzzle, your smile held me forever.
Petals blossomed, first time in life gladdened
My heart silently filled you, with a cloud of dreams,
Is it a hidden treasure inside?
What is the glitter in those eyes?
That makes me feel so much alive.
You are like dusk in the mist of day time,
You cleared all my illusions towards the life.
My foot print do you see,
How lucky you are to walk beside him.
White flowers glade sill on the side of the hill,
As sunset sweeps the scene, you shower me with your love.
In the moon light with you, what an enlivened delighted!
I hold those pieces of my broken colorful bangles,
 As a memory in the blue night, bathed the silver moonlight.

Lord, Protector and Provider

By Melissa Meeks

Ensconced in Your embrace, I'm securely concealed
Your sanctuary high above shelters me from harm
My weary soul soaks in sustenance and renewal
Amidst the secluded retreat of Your presence

Dense, forbidding stone masks lush, peaceful meadows
Where Your children delight in unique fellowship
Guests are overwhelmed by blessings beyond human grasp
Your ever open arms beckon us to a much needed refuge.

Elusive Love

By Margaret Peterson

"Fresh Florals. Good morning, this is Corrine. How may I help you?" She picked up a pencil. "Yes…we do…dozen…what color? Certainly, sir. What is your phone number? Was that 28? Thank you. What shall I put on the card? Please spell that name. Yes, I'll put "with love"."

Love, love, love. She was surrounded by it, but it eluded her.

She completed writing the order and went to the back room of the shop. She reached for a delicate glass vase as the door signal interrupted her with an insistent 'jing jing'. She returned to see a young man, about her age, wearing a gray wool topcoat. He removed his leather gloves and gave a smile that entranced her.

"I'm here for the carnations for my mom. I called on Saturday and was told they would be ready Monday morning."

She smiled and nodded. "I'll get them for you." She returned to the back to wrap cellophane around pink and white carnations that stood in a metal bucket. A lacy ribbon secured the flowers and she tied it using the intricate bow her boss had demonstrated when Corrine had started at the store two years ago. She had envisioned opportunities to meet people, to be honest, men, when she was hired, not to learn how to tie fancy bows. This latest customer looked promising.

He wasn't. "My wife was going to pick these up, but she got called into work."

Corrine forced a smile and went through the routine like a robot. He left with another engaging smile. Her shoulders sagged. She sighed and returned to the other room. She yanked aside a clump of chrysanthemums to reach the roses and grabbed a pair of scissors. Yet another brief hope had fizzled.

The expectations she held for the men she dated had met the same fate. They were pleasant company; some strikingly handsome, but all without charisma. There was never a spark from any of them to set her heart aflame. At twenty-seven Corrine was getting desperate.

She snipped at rose stems absently and remembered how she had toyed with the idea of an online dating service. It came with a promise to meet one's 'soul mate' there. Unsettling stories from friends who had tried this route turned her off. Still, they had somehow found husbands.

With each wedding invitation she felt more like the last kid picked on a team.

*****

At the latest reception Corrine had admired the flower arrangement at the head table.

"When is it going to be your turn to be a bride, my dear?"

At her aunt's voice she squared her shoulders and faced the woman, "Good question."

Her aunt frowned. "You should have been married by…."

Corrine interrupted, "Aren't these beautiful blossoms?"

"Don't change the subject." Her aunt shook her finger at her niece, "Haven't you found anyone you like better than yourself?"

Corrine's face reddened as if she had been slapped. She took a deep breath, dug her fingernails into her palms and mumbled, "Excuse me," She strode away, her gown swishing about her knees. But the question pursued her. Was she that egotistical? The thought haunted her.

*****

Early the next morning she took her dog for a walk. As Buster sniffed at scents Corrine searched her soul. What was the truth? Had she been too self-focused?

At the end of the long walk she had the answer. She determined to socialize more frequently, to concentrate on others, to disregard her longings.

She joined a bowling league, volunteered at the dog shelter, took out a membership in the "Guys and Girls Hiking Club" and agreed to the blind dates her friend arranged for her. It had been a waste of her time and energy. Her quest for "Mr. Right" was still foremost in her mind. Would she ever find him?

She hated to resign herself to the single life. Having no husband, no children was unappealing; even embarrassing.

'Jing, jing.' A voice called out, "Corrine?"

"In here, Jenny."

"Thanks for opening for me today. My husband should be back tonight." She shrugged out of her coat and hung it on the hook next to Corrine's. "I sure miss him when he has to attend head office meetings. Then I have to take the kids to school too." She unwound the scarf from her neck and fluffed up her auburn curls. "Having Peter miles from here is just too far for me."

Corrine glanced up from arranging the roses in an ornate vase to see a tender look in Jenny's green eyes. Love, love, love. Like the fragrant scent of the roses she could perceive it but not retrieve it. She had to grin at the silliness of the rhyming words.

She and her boss worked side by side throughout the morning in the back room's cool atmosphere. The variety of blooms there looked like the pages of a seed catalogue in every shade of color from deepest purple to palest cream.

From them Jenny and Corrine created bouquets, corsages, basket arrangements and wreaths. They had accomplished most of the required morning's work when Jenny flicked up her jacket sleeve and checked her watch. "Hey, it's already noon. You go first for lunch."

Corrine was in the middle of arranging tulips and lilies. "No, you go ahead. I want to finish this."

"You sure?"

"Yeah."

"Okay, I won't be long." She slipped out of her peach jacket with "Fresh Florals" printed in raised gold letters on the pocket. A minute later the 'Jing, jing' told Corrine she had left.

The arrangement was coming together well; Corrine enjoyed her job. She and Jenny had become close friends. She was a frequent guest for dinner at Jenny and Peter's home as well as a favorite babysitter for their three children. She had fun as she dressed up with the girls in Jenny's old party clothes or played Checkers with their brother.

Corrine added baby's breath to the vase and reached for greenery when the door chime signaled a customer. She stepped out to see the second good looking man of the day close the door behind him. "Better keep out of the cold," he said as he turned toward her with a wide smile. "You probably hate it when anyone opens that door on a day like this."

Not when someone looks like you, she felt like saying, but she only smiled and said, "I get used to it. It's one of the reasons I like to wear this jacket."

"The color sure suits your beautiful hair."

Corrine recognized the familiar quick beat of her heart as her hopes soared. Then she glanced at the man's hand and saw a wedding ring. She lowered her head. "Thank you."

Her two years of training kicked in and she lifted her head, willed herself to smile. "How may I help you?"

When Jenny returned Corrine crossed the street to the small café where the smell of brewing coffee mixed with that of tangy chili and turkey soup enveloped her. She plopped down on a stool.

Immediately the cook came from the kitchen. Behind him, through the opening opposite the counter, several pots steamed on an immense stainless steel stove. Corrine looked up past the immaculate white coat to the chef's hat that made the man seem even taller.

"Where's Susan?"

"She got snowed in skiing on the pass this weekend so I'm doing double duty for today." Corrine remembered the plans her waitress friend had shared.

"Without her here that must be a lot of work for you." She looked into his eyes, bright blue under the starched white hat.

"It doesn't happen very often." He gave her a warm smile. Not another handsome man. Corrine could not take it. She looked at his hand; well-shaped with strong square fingers ending in short, clean nails. No wedding ring. That meant nothing; lots of married men did not wear them.

"The usual order?"

"Why, yes, but how do you know what I want?"

"I've been making your lunch for the last two years, back there." He nodded toward the kitchen, "You may not have noticed me but I sure noticed you." Another compliment, probably followed by another let down.

"I...I guess I never saw you because your back was turned most of the time."

"When I did face your way, you were always talking to Susan." He laughed in an easy going way, "Your name's Corrine, isn't it?" She nodded. "Susan has told me a lot about you."

Corrine frowned up at him. "Really?"

He cleared his throat and readjusted his hat. "Actually, it's because I asked." A dark red flush spread across his face and touched his ears.

She felt like smiling at his discomfort but she maintained her serious look. "So you know lots about me and I know nothing about you. That doesn't sound very fair, does it?" She spread her hands apart and stared at him, but then she could not hold back a smile.

"I'm Tony, I own this place and I…."

A customer interrupted him, "More coffee, please."

"Sorry," he said to her.

She watched his athletic form in the chef uniform as he left. On his return he said, "I can't talk now but if you stop in at closing time over dinner I can tell you about myself to even that unfair score."

Corrine's heart began its quick beat. She could hardly get the words out, "Sounds fair to me."

"How was lunch?" Jenny asked as Corrine removed her coat.

Corrine grinned. "I met Tony, the owner. He seemed nice."

"Yes, he and Lisa are."

"Lisa?" Corrine's demeanor crumpled. "He's married?"

"Uh uh. Lisa's his sister." Jenny snipped stems from dahlias. "My brothers and I went to school with them."

Relief flooded Corrine's face and the light returned to her eyes. "Oh."

Jenny glanced up. "His parents were good folks. Tony took over the café when his dad died."

'Jing jing.'

"I'll get it."

Corrine hummed as she picked up the next order form. She had not known a delphinium from a dandelion when she was hired but Jenny was patient and Corrine learned under her guidance. She discovered her flair for arranging and soon could send gifts of flowers to her family and her many friends.

At five-thirty Jenny tallied up the day's invoices while Corrine refreshed her make-up.

"Going somewhere after work?"

Corrine's smile was immediate. "Tony invited me for dinner."

"And you kept that a secret all afternoon?"

"It's no big deal."

"Hmm, from the look on your face I'd say it was." She gave her friend a thumbs up. "Have a good time."

"Thanks, I think I will."

She did. The dinner was cooked to perfection and Tony was charming company. After the meal he walked her to her Honda and asked her for a date for Friday night. Corrine agreed with enthusiasm.

Tony took her to a live theatre production and said he would like to see her again the next evening.

"I'd love to, but I'm babysitting for Jenny and Peter."

"How many kids do they have? I've forgotten."

"Three. Two girls, five and eight and a boy, six."

"I could give you a hand with them if you'd like."

"You'd want to do that?"

"Sure, I like kids and if I brought some freshly baked cookies I bet they'd be ok with me being there."

On Saturday night she saw that Tony was a natural with the children. She admired his patience and she and the children found his sense of humor entertaining.

In the months that followed Tony walked into Corrine's life daily and her heart followed his every footstep.

Jenny wanted all the details as did Susan, who plied Corrine with questions at every lunch hour.

"Where did Tony take you on the weekend?"

"We hiked and Tony brought baked treats, as usual. Last week he made brownies, the week before muffins and this time it was scones. I took lots of pictures. I've been into photography for years but it's better when I have Tony to share it with." She lowered her voice. "And Susan, he wanted me to meet his mom."

"Gosh, he must be serious about you."

Corrine's curls bounced on her shoulder as she nodded. "I thought the same thing." She breathed in deeply. "We got along really well."

"Who couldn't get along with you?"

"Thanks," she smiled. "Now I want my folks to meet him. They have teased me about how infrequently I stop in to visit them." She took a sip of her water. "I spend more time with Tony than I do with my dog." She snickered. "Tony is giving him stiff competition." The two friends laughed.

"You're not entering Buster in any more competitions?"

"No, I haven't even gone online to see about the next event."

Susan grinned. "Gee, I wonder why?"

When Tony and Corrine had been dating a year he wanted to celebrate with a special dinner. They discussed plans while they walked Buster and stopped for a picnic lunch. Corrine teased him, "You've run out of new things to bake, darling." She giggled and tapped his arm." This is the second time this month you've made chocolate chip cookies."

He grinned and grabbed her hand. "You're right." He brought her fingers to his lips and kissed them. "I'll order a cake for Saturday night at that new restaurant we've decided to try." He chuckled. "We'll see what the completion has to offer."

On Saturday, seated across from Tony at a table for two, Corrine gazed at the decadent masterpiece with layers of chocolate fudge that towered above a base of white chocolate. "How are we going to eat this?"

"One spoonful at a time." He handed her a spoon. "You go first."

Corrine dug into the whipped cream that covered the top layer. "Mmm." She closed her eyes in anticipation. She opened them and pulled the spoon from the frothy whiteness. Her eyebrows lifted. "Ooh."

The spoon held a blue velvet box, protected from the whipping cream by clear plastic wrapping.

Tony handed her a napkin. "Better wipe it off and open it."

Corrine's fingers trembled as she followed his directions.

She lifted the lid to reveal, encased in satin, an engagement ring. Its facets that shimmered in the table's candlelight were eclipsed by the glow in Corrine's eyes. Tony lifted the ring from the box and took Corrine's hand. "Will you marry me?"

"Yes, Tony, I will."

He slipped the ring on her finger and they both said, "I love you."

Corrine hurried to her parent's home early the following morning to share her joy. Parked in the driveway was her aunt's ancient black Cadillac.

Corrine's pace slowed. The hurtful words came as clearly as they had the first time, "Haven't you found anyone you like more than yourself?"

She thought she had dealt with them but questions overwhelmed her. Was she self-centered? Did she accept the ring only because she loved Tony or was it because she loved herself?

She turned and trudged home, her thoughts a cyclone ripping through her mind.

Her dog greeted her at the door and she knelt to hug him. "I'm so confused, Buster." She buried her face in his shaggy fur and sobbed.

At last she stood, held out her hand and stared at the gleaming diamond. It symbolized Tony's love but did it also represent her selfish goal reached?

If it did then she must return it; at once.

She rushed to Tony's café. Through the window she saw Tony preparing for the day. She banged on the glass and the smell of frying bacon accompanied his wide grin as he unlocked the door.

"Hey, what a nice surprise."

Corrine's eyes overflowed with tears. "Sweetheart, what's wrong?" He pulled her close.

"I've waited so long to be married and…."

"Those don't look like happy tears to me."

She brushed at her wet cheeks and sniffed. Tony had to bend closer to hear her words." I can't wear this ring."

"What do you mean?"

"I…I don't know." She pulled away from him. "Maybe I'm being selfish…."

"Selfish? I don't get it." Tony's brow furrowed and he rubbed his chin.

"I mean, maybe I'm wearing this ring just so I can end my quest."

"Your quest?"

"For love."

I don't understand."

"It's so complicated…I can't explain."

He took her in his arms. "You don't have to." He wiped away her fresh tears. "If you were looking for love I was seeking it, too."

Corrine's eyes widened. "You were?"

"I think everyone is." He smiled. "We were fortunate to find it."

She told him about how her aunt's comments had affected her. Tony shook his head. "Never let someone like that make you doubt yourself or spoil your happiness. We both found love and we will share it with each other all our lives."

"Oh, Tony, you're right." She snuggled further into his arms. "I love you".

The elusive love Corrine had searched for had been waiting for her all the time, across the street at Tony's café.

Doggone Deal of Love

By Catherine Mayer Donges

Megan O'Reilly never expected to find love again. In fact, she didn't even want to. Sean had been the love of her life. She never wanted anyone else; not in the 28 years they were married, nor in the 5 years since she lost him to a disease that slowly chipped away at who he was till there was nothing left but an empty shell. By the time she laid him in the ground last year, all traces of their life had been erased from his memory. He forgot her; their two children; the home that they had built together; and even their sweet little dog, Molly.

One evening as Megan was making a vain attempt at cleaning up the place, which had fallen into a state of semi-squalor since Sean died, she accidentally knocked Molly's leash off the hook by the door. As she bent down to pick it up; Molly came running from her place on the sofa and gleefully alternated between a dance and a sitting position, her tail wagging furiously in either case, obviously excited by the sound of the leash and the prospect of having the opportunity to go for a walk. "Ah Molly, poor thing, how long has it been since anyone walked you?" Megan asked as she bent down and buried her hands in the soft, auburn fur of her beloved Cocker Spaniel's neck.

A flood of memories came rushing back, matched drop for drop with the tears that began cascading down Megan's cheeks. She recalled Molly as an eight-week-old pup just learning the words heel; sit; and come, as she pranced down the street pulling Sean behind her. She recalled long walks in the park in early twilight hours and games of fetch that Molly and Sean played as they sat on their favorite bench near the lake. Then there was the last walk Sean would take Molly on. The rising panic when they didn't return home, the frantic calls she placed trying to locate her missing husband, the phone call to the police, and eventually his ominous return where she had learned the reason for their delay was that Sean had forgotten how to get home and had probably even walked past their house several times unable to recognize it.

The doctor's visits that were to follow confirmed what they both already feared, and Sean was diagnosed with early-onset Alzheimer's, the same disease that had taken his mother years earlier.

In the days to come all their shared memories became hers, and hers alone, to carry. She figured she had more than enough of them to see her through till the day when she would find him again and he would remember her name. Still, at this point in time, those memories were still too fresh. Like a skinned knee that had just been cleansed with bubbles of peroxide, they were painful. Too painful to remain focused on them day in and day out.

At first she had just buried herself in her work, offered to invest time in special projects, offered to stay late and complete tasks that could certainly wait till the next day to be done. The reality was that during the time when she was preoccupied taking care of Sean, she had made herself redundant. The tasks that had been delegated as hers alone to complete were portioned off to coworkers who absorbed the workload; it was now obvious to everyone involved that the office could function quite well without her. Still her employer was kind enough to keep her on in her time of financial need, but while he continued to pay her salary, he wasn't so gracious as to allow her overtime.

As days turned into weeks and weeks became months; clouded by the judgment of grief and depression; Megan eventually came to the conclusion that the only living, breathing being on the earth who really needed her was Molly. Here Molly sat, her pleading eyes slowly transforming into a look of resignation as her head sunk to the floor. Megan hung the leash back on the hook and sat down on the floor next to the dog in yet another bout of overwhelming grief. "Oh Molly, I am so sorry," she sobbed, "You have always been such a good girl. I know what you want, but it is just so hard." Molly looked up at her owner out of the corner of her eye before letting it all go with a huff. She sat back up and began licking the salty tears from Megan's face. Molly's willingness to forgive and forget still astounded Megan, and she took the little dog into her arms. "You are the most important thing in the world to me, do you know that?"

Oh sure, she knew that her children still cared, but they had busy lives of their own. Her son, Matthew, the older of her two children was too busy climbing the corporate ladder to find time to establish a family of his own, no less to find time for her. Sure there were the obligatory calls once a week that let her know he was still alive and thinking of her, but he had followed his dreams all the way to the West Coast. Maureen, on the other hand, lived relatively close by and was, at least, someone she could turn to in an emergency. She had already volunteered to take care of her adored grandson, Drew, over the summer during the gap between hockey camp and school's reopening in August, but during the rest of the year she was more of an interruption in their routine of homework, hockey practice and games.

Molly, on the other hand, would wait by the back door every evening in anticipation of her return. She would greet Megan gleefully and spend hours sitting by her side just enjoying her company. One evening, in a moment of desperation, Megan had contemplated the thought that everyone would be better off if she weren't around, but it was the concern of what would happen to Molly that pulled her through.

"Okay, girl, you're right. It's time I start thinking of you for a change and a walk is just what we both need to get us out of this funk." Megan stood back up and grabbed her jacket and the leash. At first, Molly hesitated. She wasn't up to having her heart broken twice in one night, but when Megan bent down and attached the leash to her collar, she quickly became the happy-go-lucky pup she had once been.

As they walked out in the cool spring air, Megan couldn't help but realize that her dog really was the perfect partner. Molly forgave her when she ran out of her favorite doggie treat and forgot to get more on the way home. Molly gleefully shared in whatever Megan decided to eat herself and never complained that the burger was burnt around the edges or the fries were too salty. Molly didn't even judge her when she put on her favorite outfit and discovered it had grown too tight from the myriads of sundaes she had consumed in front of the TV every night. Molly was perfect and she deserved better than what she had been getting recently.

The first walk was a trip around the block before Megan was too tired to go on. The next night was a little further, and the night after that, further still. Slowly her stamina increased, her mood lifted, and she began to feel more like herself than she had in a really long time. After a week and a half of jaunts around their neighborhood, Megan decided it was time for the pair to venture into the world at large. A new dog park had opened up, and she was absolutely certain Molly would love the opportunity to run and play with other four-legged people who could keep up with her. After a quick stop at the pet store to pick up a Frisbee and a ball, they set off for the park on the other side of town.

Megan was surprised at how many people, both two-legged and four, were there. Pups ran from one end of the park to the other in games of tag and keep away, while owners milled around admiring each other's companions. Molly, who hadn't been around other dogs in a really long time, glued herself to Megan's heels and refused to retrieve the Frisbee Megan threw only a few yards away. As Megan tried to coax her into going after it, a brown lab mix swooped in and scooped the Frisbee into its mouth.

"Hank, where are your manners? That doesn't belong to you," a male voice called out from the direction of the entrance before Megan had time to react.

As Megan turned toward the direction of the voice, she saw a man, about her age, attached to five leashes, each with a different type of dog attached to the end, coming through the gate. There was a poodle, a shepherd, a boxer, a Siberian husky, and a mutt so strange as to elude any form of identification as to what breed it contained. "Drop it Hank, right now." The dog ran back over to its master and gently dropped the disc at his feet. "Good boy," the man said before picking up the Frisbee and heading in her direction. "I'm really sorry ma'am. He's just enthusiastic," he said, sticking out his right hand for a shake while passing the toy to her with his left.

"That's quite alright, I understand," she replied as she brushed her sweaty hand off on her jeans before taking the man's hand. "I-um, so are all these dogs yours?" She asked, hoping not to come off as too awkward. There was something about the guy that made her stomach flutter the moment she laid eyes on him. He was shorter than Sean, but he had the same rugged build and same squared jaw line. Unlike Sean's blue eyes, the stranger's eyes were a soft, chocolate brown. He had a well-trimmed beard and a nose that turned up slightly at the end. What really got her though was his smile. He had one of those smiles that immediately disarmed any weariness and brought you into a circle of friendship. This guy had to be either a car salesman, a realtor, or an insurance guy like Sean. Whatever he was selling, she was definitely interested in buying, despite herself.

"Ah, naw," he replied to the question she had already forgotten she'd asked. "They're all shelter dogs," he replied as he unleashed the dogs and allowed them to go running off in all directions, "except Hank, he's mine."

"Shelter dogs?"

"Yeah, I volunteer down at the ASPCA as a dog walker. I go in a couple times a week and offer myself to walk dogs, clean crates, whatever they need me to do."

"Why that's very generous of you... Mr. ... I'm sorry, what did you say your name was again?" Megan felt her cheeks flush and her head grow a bit dizzy.

"Don't think I did. Allen, Allen Birmingham, and you are?"

"Megan O'Reilly, please, just call me Megan."

"Okay Megan, pleased to meet you. I'm sorry, but I'm sure I've never seen you or your pretty little dog there before? Do you come here often?"

"No, actually, today is my first time. You see my husband died a few months back, and well I've been...." Megan stopped herself from continuing, realizing she had been divulging way too much about herself to a perfect stranger.

"Been what?"

"Oh, nothing. I'm sorry Mr. Birmingham, I mean Allen. You don't need to know about my troubles."

"Are you sure? I can be a pretty good listener." Obviously sensing her discomfort, he gracefully changed the subject. "Well look at that.... Seems like my Hank is taking quite a shining to your.... I'm sorry, I didn't catch your dog's name."

"Molly, her name's Molly."

"Well it seems that Hank has found himself quite smitten with your Molly."

Megan looked back over her shoulder in time to see Molly nip at Hank's heels, race off a short distance, then turn back around and run circles around Hank. He got down on his forepaws and stuck his butt up in the air. His tail was wagging furiously.

"So he has, and it seems like she is taken with him also." Megan's stomach did another flip as the unspoken words between them created a mild awkwardness she hadn't felt since she was a teenager. "So, Allen, what do you do for a living when you're not walking dogs or cleaning up poop?"

"I'm a minister. Presbyterian. And you?"

Megan had been totally unprepared for his response and given her response earlier, a bit embarrassed by her thoughts. Then again, he was a salesman of sorts. "Me, I-um-I'm a secretary, well an executive assistant, I guess is the term used now-a-days. I used to be a teacher, but I stopped teaching when my children were born and stayed home and taught them. By the time I was ready to go back, teaching jobs had become a scarcity."

"I understand. You're probably better off. From what I hear teaching isn't what it used to be. The kids just don't respect their teachers like they used to. Their ministers either, for that matter."

"I suppose you're right. She glanced down at his hands, and not seeing a ring, she dared to ask the one question she was dying to know. So, well, I already blurted out that I'm a widow. So what about you? Are you married?"

"Me, naw. Not now anyway. Not in quite a while. Since before I joined the ministry, actually. My wife, well let's just say I wasn't the man I am today, and she found herself somebody who could love her in a way I couldn't at the time."

"Oh, well, I'm sorry."

"Sorry for what? It probably was the best thing that ever happened to me, to tell the truth. I used to be a drinker. Her leaving sobered me up. Haven't had a drink in more than 20 years. Found a calling. Life's all good." He had made eye contact and didn't break it the entire time he was speaking. "So how long were you married?"

"Twenty eight years, going on twenty nine. He died last year of Alzheimer's."

"Man that's rough."

"Yeah, it really was. He was such a good man. Kind, loving, and then almost overnight all he was as a man, as a husband, started slipping away. By the time he died, he had no idea who I was."

"In my line of work, I've witnessed it happen a time or two. For the family, sometimes at the end, it's almost a relief."

She couldn't believe he had just said that. Lord help her, the thought had crossed her mind a time or two, but she would never have dared to put those thoughts into words. Not then, not now, maybe not ever. "I'm sorry.... It's getting late. I think it's time for Molly and I to get on home. Molly...."

"I'm sorry. I didn't mean to offend...."

"No, really, you didn't. It's okay, but I really need to be going. It was nice meeting you Pastor Birmingham, really. I.... Molly!" Molly returned and Megan wasted no time attaching the leash and beating a hasty retreat. She was in the car and exiting the parking lot before she realized that she had forgotten the ball and Frisbee. "Damn.... I'm sorry Molly. I'll get you replacements," she said as though the dog would have been upset at her carelessness at leaving the toys behind.

It was three days before she even allowed herself to think about what occurred between her and the minister. By that time, she had come to the conclusion that she had over-reacted and embarrassed herself once again. It took a week before she had the courage to keep her promise to Molly to take her back to the park and then only because she figured that her chance encounter had been a fluke, and it was highly unlikely that she would run into him again. For the next two visits, it appeared that she was right, but on the third return visit she found herself face to face with him once again.

"Hank and I have been worried about you two," he said as he approached her directly. "I thought maybe I had permanently scared you away."

"Who me, oh no. You didn't do anything wrong. I... I've just been really busy, and we've just been missing each other is all." Megan suddenly realized she didn't want to lie to him. She wasn't sure if that was because of his profession or because there was something that told her she should trust him. "Well, to be perfectly honest, I wasn't ready to talk about my feelings when Sean died."

"And now?"

"Now I think I need to admit the truth to myself and to you."

"I see, and what is that truth?"

"You were right. By the time Sean died, I had realized that what had happened to him wasn't suddenly going to change. He wasn't going to suddenly start remembering me again. He wasn't going to get any better. It was time to let him go. Doing so meant relief for him and for me."

"It isn't unusual to feel that way. That was what I was trying to tell you."

"I know, but it still felt wrong somehow."

"How we feel isn't necessarily good or bad. It just is."

"That is rather existential coming from a man of the cloth, don't you think?"

"How so?" he asked as he put his hand to his chin, reminding Megan of the statue "The Thinker."

"According to the Bible we are very much responsible for our negative feelings and thoughts. The seven deadly sins; envy, lust, pride and all that." Megan ticked them off on her fingers as she tried to recall exactly what they were.

"Actually, the seven deadly sins aren't in the Bible." He cocked his head and grinned in a way that was both charming and disarming.

"Oh?" Megan raised her eyebrows as a sign of skepticism.

"They are actually part of Catholic Catechism."

"Well at least I heard it somewhere." Megan bit her lower lip. She probably should have known better than to discuss religious and Biblical philosophy with a man who had spent so much time studying it. She had to admit, at least to herself, that Bible reading wasn't part of her regular repertoire. As a Catholic, she took what she was taught at face value and didn't question whether it was actually Biblical or not. But even as a Catholic, she wasn't exactly practicing. She couldn't remember the last time she had actually been in a church, outside of Sean's funeral.

"Lust, on the other hand is mentioned in Matthew 5:27-28 in regard to the desire to possess another man's wife. The passage has been much debated."

"Is that the verse about 'a man lusting after a woman has already sinned in his heart'?"

"Something like that." He shook his head a bit and grinned out of the right side of his mouth. He obviously liked having the philosophical advantage. "In any event, there are those that believe that if Jesus actually said it. Even if he did, he wasn't condemning anyone for having a dirty thought on occasion."

"And you sir, have you ever had such a thought?" Megan was sure that asking such a question was a way of leveling the playing field. He was a man after all, and what red-blooded man hadn't had such a thought or two. It served him right for making fun of her.

"Actually, I am having such a thought right now." He hadn't missed a beat and burst into a full out laugh as her cheeks blazoned fire red.

"Pastor Birmingham…." was all she could say before covering her face with her hands.

"Well I'm really glad we've run in to each other today," he said, changing the subject.

"I guess you are!"

"Well sure, remember Hank was absolutely smitten. He has been beside himself since."

"Oh, really?"

"Look at the two of them."

Megan tried hard to stifle her tendency to want to grin, but she had to admit that it appeared he was right. Molly and Hank only seemed to have eyes, or at least noses, for each other and were busy engaging in a rousing game of tag, with her leading him on and him in hot pursuit. "So it seems."

" So, what do you say to our stopping for a cup of coffee after their game?"

"I don't know…. I mean I really don't like leaving Molly in the car."

"Who said anything about leaving her in the car. We can go someplace that has outdoor seating, a drive through, it doesn't really matter to me."

"Well, I don't know. It's still kind of cool out."

"I'll keep you warm…. I mean the coffee or maybe hot chocolate…. my treat. Please, let me make it up to you for putting my foot in my mouth multiple times."

Megan's stomach did another flop at the innuendo of the first part. "There's nothing to make up, really. We're fine. I… I'd like that… the coffee I mean."

"Good, then it's a date, well not a real date, but…."

"Pastor Birmingham, I do believe you are almost as easy to fluster as I am."

"Okay, well I'm going to go out on a limb here. Okay, bear with me. It's been a really long time since I've done this, and I probably wasn't very good at it even back then. I can't remember when the last time I even thought about wanting to get to know a woman better. I mean…. I get to know lots of people. It's my job, but it's been a long time since I wanted to…."

"Okay, okay…. Let's just say that I'm interested in getting to know you too."

"Fine then, but let's get one thing straight, right from the start."

"Oh…kaaay…."

"I'm Allen, just plain old Allen. No more Pastor Birmingham, please. Deal?"

"Deal, Allen."

One coffee date led to another, and it wasn't long before she was cooking him dinner. He took her to the movies and bowling. It was an old-fashioned courtship. Until it wasn't.

Megan was more than a bit distressed when he didn't call as he had promised on their last evening together. At first she was worried, then she was mad. But when he didn't show up at the dog park for an entire week in a row, Megan knew something had gone very wrong. She kept racking her brain trying to figure out what had happened. She wondered if she had unintentionally done or said something that scared him off. She couldn't figure it out. She hoped to find him at the dog shelter. Her heart broke when she learned about Hank.

Apparently, one of Allen's neighbors had put rat poison in their can. Hank had gotten out when Allen opened the door for a parishioner, and before he could stop him, Hank had attacked the garbage can. According to the manager of the shelter, Allen was beating himself up for not realizing what Hank had eaten. By the time he realized something was wrong, Hank was having seizures. He later slipped into a coma. While the emergency vet where Hank was being treated was doing everything in their power to save him, the longer Hank was unconscious, the less likely it was that anything would work.

After securing the address of the vet from the manager, Megan drove directly there. If Allen was anything like her, she knew he probably hadn't eaten or slept since Hank had been admitted. She knew how much Allen loved Hank and was sure this was the case. As she entered the hospital waiting room, she knew she was right. Allen was sitting in the corner staring off into space. He didn't even seem to notice her. He obviously hadn't shaved, and there were dark circles under his eyes. She sat beside him and took his hand.

It was only then that he looked up at her. "Megan, what are you doing here?"

"Oh Allen, I came as soon as I heard. I am so sorry. How is Hank doing? Is there anything I can do?"

Allen shook himself free of her and stood looking out the window. "Yeah, you can go home."

"Excuse me." Megan couldn't believe his tone was actually rude.

"I'm sorry. I... I... look, there isn't anything anyone can do right now." He turned back toward her. "This is all too painful. I know that I am being unreasonable, given that you lost your husband and compared to losing him a dog is nothing, but...."

"But nothing. That dog was, is your family. Don't you think I know that? It isn't unreasonable to be out of your mind with worry.... Why if anything ever happened to Molly...." Megan didn't try to hide the tears that were running down her cheeks.

"Thank you. I appreciate that you understand, really I do, but I really want you to go home. Spend time with Molly. Hug her. Play with her. Shower her with all the love and affection I know you feel for her. I promise I'll call you if anything changes." He sat back down in the chair opposite her and put his head in his hands.

"Okay, if that is what you really want. She fell to her knees and put her hand on his shoulder.

"It is," he said, not moving in response to her touch.

As she got back into her car, Megan couldn't help but feel like their exchange had been somewhat surreal. They had been so close over the past several weeks, and now suddenly he was treating her like a stranger. Apparently, she had totally misjudged things. She had emotionally taken things much further along than he had ever intended. The fact that she couldn't trust her own judgment was more than a little bit unsettling. Was she really that desperate for a man in her life that she would fall for the first guy who paid her even the least bit of attention? He was right. Her priority needed to be the one being that really did care about her. Molly. Sweet, adorable little Molly was who really mattered. To hell with Pastor Allen Birmingham. She had let her guard down and he had forgotten her as fast as she could blink her eyes. Just like Sean had, but at least Sean had an excuse.

She started the engine and drove off in a puff of exhaust as large as the billowing smoke that would be expected from the explosion of all her dreams. To hell with all of them. She promised herself there and then that no man, no human would ever get close enough to hurt her like that again. It just wasn't worth it.

Megan had been home three hours before she noticed the on-off flicker of the voicemail on her phone. Without giving it much thought, she pressed the button and immediately heard Allen's voice. "Hello Megan, you're not going to believe…."

Her first reaction was to erase the message without waiting to hear what he had to say, but as she reached for the erase button, she saw Molly sitting up, ears perked, at the sound of his voice. Images of Hank and Molly frolicking in the park flashed before her. She sighed and continued to listen.

"…this. Hank's awake. The doctors came out and told me they think he's going to be okay. It's a miracle, Meg. I can't tell you how relieved I am. I'll be here for another hour or two, but the doctor says I should go home and rest. If all goes well, they may actually be discharging Hank as early as tomorrow. Call me. Okay. Love you. Bye.

Had her ears deceived her? Had he actually said he loved her? He probably wasn't thinking. It was just one of those things you kind of say before you hang up with someone you know. If he really loved her, he wouldn't have pushed her away the way he did. If he really loved her, he wouldn't have broken her heart the first time something difficult came up. No, she couldn't allow him to hurt her again. It was better this way, but she should at least respond so that he wouldn't keep trying to call. Instead of picking up the landline, she went and fetched her cell phone out of her purse. She tried hard to ignore the silly banter that had been part of their last text session, instead she simply wrote: I'm glad Hank is okay. Molly misses him. She pressed the send icon and dropped the cell back into her purse.

If she thought the brevity of her message would be enough to end the conversation and prevent him from trying to contact her again, she was sorely mistaken. There were at least a half dozen phone messages, a dozen texts, several apologies, and a dozen roses at her doorstep that said otherwise. She ignored them all, except for the roses. Those she refused to take from the delivery boy. She felt this would finally be enough for him to get the message that she wasn't interested in picking up where they left off.

The doorbell rang at six that evening. Megan looked through the keyhole and there he stood with the same dozen roses in his arms, along with a white flag. Her first reaction was to not open the door, but her car was in the driveway. It wasn't long before his persistence had outdone hers. He had been pressing her doorbell nonstop for the past five minutes, and if the sound of the infernal buzzing wasn't enough, Molly had been barking her head off for the same amount of time.

She finally unbolted the door and turned the knob. He pushed past her, dropping the flowers in her arms as he did. "Look, Megan, we need to talk…."

"What is there to talk about? You are a smart man, Rev. Birmingham. I would have thought you had gotten the message by now that we have nothing to talk about. We are done. Now, please, take your flowers and leave. She pushed the bouquet back at him and pricked herself on a thorn as she did. "Ouch."

"I'm not leaving here till you hear me out."

"If you don't leave here now, I am calling the police," she bluffed.

"Go right ahead, I am not leaving." He dropped the flowers on her coffee table and sat on the couch, folding his right leg over his left knee, before sitting back with his arm stretched across the back.

"Fine. Say what you came to say and go." She refused to give him the satisfaction of sitting.

He uncrossed his legs and sat forward. "I came to tell you that I'm sorry. I'm sorry I pushed you away when you were only trying to help."

"Fine, you're forgiven. Now leave."

"I also came to tell you that I was scared. I thought I was about to lose Hank, and I, a minister, who is supposed to help others through these types of things, couldn't help myself. I sat there, minute after minute, hour after hour, day after day, alone…."

"And whose fault is that?"

"Mine, okay, it was mine. All I kept thinking was that this was too painful. If loving meant such pain, then I didn't want to love anymore. Not the dogs at the shelter, not Molly, not even you. It was just safer not to get too close. Haven't you ever felt that way?"

Megan took in a deep breath and exhaled before turning around. "Yes, Allen, I have."

"Then why can't you forgive me?"

The question was a good one. He deserved a good answer, but at the moment she couldn't give him one. She just stood there wondering to herself why she hadn't reacted more positively than she had to his reaffirming that he loved her. No matter how much she wanted to erase the pain their last conversation had caused her, she couldn't. He had reminded her how dangerous love was. The reality is that no one ever lives happily ever after, not in the real world. In the real world, love hurts. Sooner or later one of the partners leaves the other, whether they want to or not. Even loving Molly was dangerous for her. Sooner or later, even Molly would leave, just as Hank almost left Allen. It was only a matter of time, but at least Molly hadn't done anything to hasten the inevitability.

"Look Allen, I do forgive you okay, but the reality is that I did realize we had taken it too fast. Way too fast. Can't we just go back to being friends?" she said as she flopped in the chair opposite him.

"But I…." He pulled a small black box from his pocket.

She flew across the room and put her hands over his, preventing him from opening it. "See! That is exactly what I mean. We haven't known each other for more than a few months, and you are already thinking marriage. God, Jesus, Allen, we aren't kids anymore. We don't just fall in and out of love at a drop of a hat. Love is a full time commitment!"

"Don't you think I know that? Don't you understand that I know full well the risks of making such a commitment? I haven't taken this step with anyone else in more than 20 years."

"But then why now? Why me?"

"Because you're different. I know that I can trust you not to hurt me."

"The way you hurt me." The words of her sentence hung in the air like a smelly cigar.

"Okay, I get it. I really do. If you want to take it slower, I can live with that. I am a patient man, but there is only one thing."

"What is that?"

"You promised to call me Allen and not Pastor, Reverend, or any other title, Birmingham."

"You are right. I did, Allen," she said as she stuck out her hand and offered to shake.

He took her hand and pulled her into a hug. "I will convince you my intentions are honorable," he whispered in to her ear. "I am patient, persistent, and persuasive. You will see."

And see she did. A year later, she finally allowed him to open the box, to put the antique diamond ring on her finger. A year after that, she followed Hank and Molly down the aisle of his church; and with a fellow pastor officiating, she allowed him to put a small band of gold on that same finger. By that time, she had realized that sometimes the risk is worth it, that not giving in to love was ultimately more painful than accepting that it is all just a part of the deal.

Wishbone in Moonglow

By Mary Langer Thompson

I leave you to the doctors
and nurses,
come home to our dark kitchen
that dry, brittle wishbone
still on the counter,
illuminated by a moonbeam.

We were going to split it to-
gether, but not now.
And anyway, it seems silly
to pull in opposite directions
as though rivals.

I step closer.
The bone's shape is an open heart,
and I know
that I want for you
what you need for me
what we hope for each other
until the clouds cover the moon forever-
that the light not leave us
tonight.

Passion Rising
By Delfin Espinosa

He looked in her eyes with desire
and in her heart he lit a fire.
He held her in his arms so tight
in her soul she felt great delight.
As they sat by the fireplace
the passion began to give chase.
Her lips were as red as wine
as he whispered in her ear be mine.
They kissed and the passion became a burning flame
to them it was all the same.
Their love for each other was incredible
the heat of passion rising was inevitable.

Unembraceable You

By Mary Langer Thompson

We found you in the attic of our house,
a stunning goddess of love and beauty.
I noticed you were in need of a blouse.
To tell your story, Mom felt her duty:

Venus emerged from sea foam to our shores.
I would later learn how that froth was born.
Adored, worshipped, you helped men win wars.
But we stole, looted, and battered your form.

A peasant named Yorgos found you one day.
Sailors dragged you across rocks to their ship,
from Milos, where you in dusty ruin lay.
You lost two appendages on that trip.

Now armless, resigned, you remain alone,
unable to grasp what begins at home.

Searching
By Melissa Meeks

Is any way clear ere I reach the goal?
Though only one course as a labyrinth
The serpentine way leaves this traveler wondering whether I come or go.
Ever an elusive goal hovering on my minds periphery
Draws my dreamer's imagination into its midst.
As I finally navigate those final feet
Desires I refused to hope could be
Are revealed as His purpose, His gift to me
From the day He "wrote" my life into being.

A blessing waiting for His timing
To brighten a road of stress and trial.
Preparing me for the story of a life
Which will somehow touch others around me.
Supporting and encouraging through circumstances
Seeming interminable as they mount one on another.

Though each of us treads a unique path
His ultimate desire is for companionship from us.
He wishes us the joy of life that things and money can never provide.
Love and provision He possesses in abundance.
They will never be depleted
He must confer them on His creation.
We then reciprocate and reflect these qualities
For struggling companions along our route.

Night's Wish
By Kimberly M. Heindorf

The tides were low and steady, making the ship rock back and forth slightly. I stood on the quarter deck; watching my men below me work vigorously.

"Which direction Captain?" my first mate of the Night's Wish, Trenton, asked.

Trenton Saltman was a decent man in his mid-thirties. Honestly, I have no idea why he chose this way of life. He was too pure for our cut throat ways. I think he liked to serve as my conscious and that's why he stuck around. Or maybe it was just a sense of loyalty.

I've known him since I was a girl. He was a teenager living off of pennies in a large port town when my father found him. My father, being the tender man he was, took Trenton in. But it wasn't my father who took him under his wing. It was my father's first mate who showed him the ropes. I couldn't have asked for a better man to run my ship.

"North, to Cammerbridge. We're going to need more supplies if we're going to find The Earlman's Chest."

"Ma'am," a crewmember said to me as he walked up the wooden steps, "will we get rum too?"

I laughed, "Of course, Gibbons."

He let out a loud whoop and ran down the stairs. He ran into Dreven, who was mopping a section where our new errand boy had gotten sea sick, and he started hugging him. Gibbons didn't even notice that he was splashing his boots in the lad's vomit. I turned to Trenton with a grimace.

"Does the crew really need any more rum?" Trenton asked while turning the wheel to the left a bit.

I gave a little sigh. I would prefer it if they didn't drink so much, but it kept them from questioning my leadership too much.

Female captains just weren't heard of and heaven help those who think that they would fit the position better.

"You know it keeps them happy," I replied to Trenton.

I could see him shaking his head from the corner of my eye.

"If you want me to replace some of these men then go out and find me some good men who won't try to sabotage or attempt to overthrow me," I snapped.

Trenton has been on my case lately to replace some of the men. They were lazy and quite possibly still sleeping in their quarters. I would love nothing more than to get rid of them, but it was hard enough to find men who would want to come aboard my ship.

Before Trenton could reply one of the men shouted, "Land!"

All the men on deck rushed to the side to look out. Land was right. Seagulls hovered around the coast of the island.

"Captain, that's Cammerbridge there," Trenton said.

I gave him a quick nod and hurried to my captain's quarters. I entered through my office. Walking past the large oak desk and the table and chairs in the corner, I went through the door that led straight to my room. Once I was inside I went to my tall, dark-cherry colored wardrobe. I found a simple low-cut blue dress hanging inside. This would do. I quickly tore off my breeches, shirt, and vest. I took off the binding around my chest before I slid on the dress. Without the binding you could see the full curves of my breasts. I smoothed the dress out; making sure it hugged what it was there for, my curves. I strapped my baldric around my waist and sheathed my weapons. Tugging on my proper ladies boots, I went out to join my crew.

I heard a few whistles as I joined them on deck. I ignored them. We were already anchored and ready to go.

"Gibbons, Lennord, and Stirnly! You're with me," I called out.

I left with the sound of Trenton ordering the men around ringing in my ears.

There were many people on the docks. Women and men. Adults and children. Didn't matter who they were. They were speeding off to their next destination.

"Come along now! Jenkins is over here," I called to my men as I walked to the shop's door.

A bell dinged as I opened up the door. I paused, causing Gibbons to ram into my back. There wasn't old man Jenkins standing behind the counter. It was a young man who looked to be about in his mid-twenties. Possibly only a few years older than me. His shoulder length black hair was slicked back into a pony tail. He had a light layer of shadow that laid upon the bottom half of his face. How he, or any man, could keep their beards that closely shaven was lost on me.

"Who are you? Where is Jenkins?" The man looked up at my voice.

His shocking blue-grey eyes sent a jolt through me.

"Jenkins left his shop to me. What can I help you with?" his silky, deep voice said.

His eyes stayed on my face; never once did they stray farther than my neck. I almost didn't know how to handle it. He needed to be interested for this to work.

I took a silent breath and finally walked forward. I used my elbow to brush back some coiled up rope and I leaned against the counter. I slid my arm under my breasts, pushing them up, and I grinned like a siren.

"I need a few things."

"Don't forget about the rum!" One of my men, Gibbons most likely, shouted behind me.

"And rum." I rolled my eyes.

"Well, what do you need?" The new merchant asked, sounding bored.

My grin widened and I reached out to stroke his arm. I needed him to drop the prices on what I was about to ask for. Jenkins was always so moldable in my palms.

"I need three barrels of fruit, seven barrels of clean water, four barrels of meat, any kind. We're not picky. And five barrels of rum. Rope. All the rope you have. A few things of oil. Some dozen candles. And you have parchment and ink, yes? I'm going to need some of that as well."

"For all that, miss, it will be 2000 gold," he said.

I figured that much. I brought that much. But it still wasn't good enough.

"2000? That's a bit steep. I could go somewhere else and get double that for the price you're asking for."

He pulled his arm away from my roaming hand.

"Sorry, Succubus, but no can do."

I shot back. With a growl I reached to my gun and I pulled it out of its holster. Pointing it at him, I gritted out, "Who are you, really? And how do you know who I am?"

Succubus of the Sea is a name I acquired back when I was just fifteen when I had discovered that men liked the new features that I had recently been forced upon. I embraced the title, but still worked hard to be unknown, unrecognizable. No one should be able to know who I really was. But he did.

"Now miss, is there any reason for that?" he gestured to my gun.

I took a glance behind me to see my men were tense and had their cutlasses drawn.

"I don't know, you tell me. Now answer my questions."

"My name is Ethan and I know that you're looking for Earlman's Chest."

I worked hard to mask my surprise. No one but my crew knew what we were searching for.

"Gibbons! Get him! Lennord and Stirnly! Help him," I commanded.

Gibbons rushed past me, but Ethan was quicker. He was running through the back of the shop.

Sighing, I grabbed some rope off the counter and ran back out the front door.

I raced through the alleys, my feet making clapping sounds caused by the short heels of my boots. I could see the blurred figures of the four men. Turning left, I sped down a thinning alley way between two building, until I turned right and jumped onto a surprised looking Ethan.

After we collapsed onto the ground and I had him pinned beneath me, I took my knife out and pointed it at his throat.

"There was no point in running," I said out of breath.

Ethan hissed in pain; he landed hard. He started to thrash under me and I dug my knife in a little deeper, piercing his skin and making little droplets of blood flow.

"Help me keep him still. I'm going to tie him up," I told my men.

They pulled him up and I worked to tie his hands tightly behind his back.

"I'm going to take him back to the ship. You three go back and gather all the supplies you can find in that shop."

"Put him down below," I said to the first man I came to when we finally reached my ship. Ethan gave no more struggles after I parted ways with my men back at Jenkin's.

I turned to Trenton, who had just come up behind me.

"Captain! What is this?" He questioned.

"Oh. That's the new merchant," I said in an innocent voice and batted my eyelashes a little. I knew my charms didn't work on Trenton. And that was fine, but we weren't having this conversation in front of my crew. Nodding my head towards my captain's quarters, I told him to follow me.

I opened the door and went straight to my desk. Collapsing in my chair, I put my feet on my desk and slouched.

"The new merchant? Are you serious? Did you have to kidnap him?"

"He wouldn't cut the prices," I said simply.

I took out my dagger and started to clean my nails with it.

"Cut- oh for the love of God! Is that it, really?"

I sighed and laid the knife down on the desk.

"He knew about the chest," I said as I folded my hands against my stomach and stared ahead.

"The chest? As in Earlman's Chest? How?"

"I don't know. But I plan on figuring that out after I get dressed."

Trenton just stared at me. His face was filled with concern and skepticism.

"Trenton? You can leave now," I said as I made a shooing motion.

Trenton nodded and swiftly left my cabin.

I shook my head and turned my attention back to my closet. I pulled out some dark brown breeches and a cream colored loose shirt.

I didn't like being around my men too much in dresses. I liked to be dressed more like them. I'd like to think that maybe if I look a little more like them they'll give me the same respect as they would give each other. I dressed quickly and tied a scarf around my head; tying a knot at the bottom of my neck. It felt nice to get the curls out of my face.

I stepped out of my cabin and walked over to the steps that led down stairs. Crates and a few dozen barrels filled up the lower deck. I could see Lennord carrying in a large barrel over his shoulder. Thank God we found him when we did. He had the strength of no man I've ever seen. He was truly a blessing to have on the ship.

Rope and other objects hung off the ceiling. I turned the corner and saw three large human sized cages. Ethan was in the last one. His arms were lazily hung out of the cage and his head was resting against the cage. I stood in front of him with my hands on my hips. He didn't look up. He just kept staring at the floor.

"How do you know about Earlman's chest?" I asked firmly.

He finally looked at me.

"I believe the question is, how do you know?"

"I asked you first."

He kept his mouth closed. I reached a hand to my cutlass and he finally spoke up. "I know all the people who are after the chest."

"Oh? And how is that?"

He didn't answer. I was getting angry again. I reached for the door and unlocked it. Ethan backed up a bit as I opened it.

I walked up to him until a whisper of wind could barely fit between us. It was hard to seem superior when he was at least a head taller.

"How?" I demanded.

"I am Earlman."

Silence filled the space around us and then I burst out laughing. Him? This fool is Earlman? I put my hand on his chest to keep me sturdy as I bent over laughing.

I stopped laughing and looked back up at him. He was looking down my shirt. I automatically straightened and put a foot between us.

"Well now you decide to pay attention to my physique," I said and crossed my arms over my chest.

"How can a man not notice you?"

"You didn't seem to notice earlier."

"It wouldn't be professional to admire a body during work."

I raised an eyebrow. "So you're a gentleman?"

"Not in the least."

He tried to step up to me, but I pulled out my cutlass and pointed it at him. He backed up a few paces and held his hands up. Slowly, he reached over and pulled up his sleeve.

A skull with a snake's tongue was shown. There was something written on the tongue. It read 'Earlman'.

My eyes widened and my breath caught. Did I really catch-

"My name is Ethan Earlman."

"How? You're so young!"

He slowly lowered his hands until they were hanging by his sides. "How long ago did you hear about the chest?"

"Only a few years ago," I replied.

"Have you ever wondered why you suddenly heard about a chest filled with great riches? And why it's taking so long to find it?"

I scrunched up my face in confusion.

"It's not real."

"You're lying!" I accused.

"I'm not. I created it to divert attention. I've been looking for something else. I wanted to search for it on my own. I sent my men out west to make the public think I was on my way to hide something. So they're following my crew while I find Deathman's Chest."

I was speechless. This young man created a great plan. There was one flaw though. He just told me his plans.

"Why are you telling me this?"

"I finally have a lead, but I need a ship. Since mine isn't available, I've had to find another one. Old man Jenkins? Yeah. He's one of mine. He told me of you. He said you have a bit of a loose tongue and had spoken of interest a while back of Earlman's Chest. He's on my ship right now."

"What? Jenkins is a pirate, your pirate, and he gave you the idea to use my ship? How exactly do you think you're going to use my ship? Do you plan on overthrowing me? Take my ship and I will gut you," I threatened.

"I'm not going to take your ship. I merely want your help. And I'll give you half of Deathman's treasure."

Was it worth the risk? He could be lying. About any of it. But it was Deathman. One of the largest pirate treasure's.

"Fine. You've got yourself a deal." I sheathed my cutlass. "Welcome aboard the Night's Wish, Mr. Earlman. You better hope we find this treasure, otherwise you'll be thrown overboard to swim with the sharks."

*****

It's been two months since I've welcomed Ethan aboard The Night's Wish. He swears that we're getting closer. He said the chest is hidden on an island off the coast of the new Americas. We've passed the Americas a few days ago. The island he speaks of should be coming up soon.

Ethan seemed to fit right in with my crew. He was outgoing, cheerful, and a down-right scoundrel. Thanks to Trenton's ears, I knew he had a bet going on with most of my men about if and when he can make it back to my bed.

It had been about two weeks ago when it happened. Ethan was making suggestive comments and I flirted back. He made me feel good with his words and I stroked his ego every once in a while.

Then one day we got into a fight.

"You said we'd be there in a few weeks. It's been almost two months!" I all but screamed.

We were in my office and Trenton stood silently in the corner as Ethan and I had a screaming match.

"It has only been a few weeks! It's just past the Americas and we're passing them right now!"

"You specifically told me a few weeks! A few weeks does not mean six weeks. That's more than a few!"

"Lord! May I remind you that we were just in a storm a few weeks ago that took some time to pass through? You must be really bored if you're blasting off about how long it takes to get there."

"I'm not bored!" I scoffed.

"Oh, really?" His eyes scanned down and landed on my chest, which was heaving. I could see, feel the heat in his stare. "I could give you something to do."

"You couldn't handle it," I taunted.

"Try me."

As I started to give him a devilish grin, Trenton gave a cough.

"Captain, if I may speak to you privately." He looked at Ethan and nodded his head to the door.

Ethan gave a mock salute and left.

"Esmine. If I may be so bold, I don't think you should do that to Ethan."

I placed my hands on my hips. "Do what?"

"Egg him on. You see, there's a bet going on." He paused, almost as if he didn't want to say anymore.

"What bet?" I growled.

"The men have bets on how long it will take Ethan to make his way back to your bed."

I scowled. Of course they did. It didn't surprise me really. I knew that all these men were scoundrels. Every last one of them, Ethan included. But there was no way in hell that I was inviting Ethan back to my bed now.

Ever since then he's been flirting like mad. He's actually very good at it. There were a few times where I considered taking him back to my quarters since then.

But then I remember the bet. And that all his flirting isn't because he actually likes me, but because he fancies what pennies he can gather from the men. I wouldn't allow him the satisfaction.

Shaking my head, I paid attention to the horizon. I heard a cry of a seagull.

"Captain, they're flying West," Trenton said.

"Yes," I agreed. West was the direction we were headed. And if there were birds flying that way it meant there was somewhere for them to land.

About two hours later, Trenton and I heard Gibbons yell, "Land!"

*****

"I told you this island exists," Ethan said next to me.

I shot him a glare. "You didn't mention that you didn't know which island it was on."

There were eight islands and he had sheepishly admitted that he didn't know which one the treasure resided on.

It would take us weeks to scour every inch of every island. No, not weeks. Months, really.

Turning around away from the islands I called out, "Saltman! Captain's Quarters now!" I turned to Ethan. "You're coming too."

We stood around the table looking at Ethan's rough sketch of the islands.

"So how are we going to do this?" I asked them.

Trenton leaned over the map to get a better look.

"It would take too long to search each island individually,"

I nodded in agreement. "What if I split up the men? I make groups and each group will search an island. Trenton, you can stay here and man the ship. I'll leave a few men with you so if anything goes wrong you can send them out."

"What if the men find nothing?" Trenton asked.

"Well then I'll just have to search every island myself."

"What about him?" Trenton nodded to Ethan.

He still didn't trust him fully. Good. Neither did I.

"Oh, he's coming with me."

We worked for the next half hour grouping men and sending them off to their islands. I assigned Gibbons, Lynch, Manolo, Ethan, and myself to the sixth island.

"I'll send someone to you if the men find something. Or if there's trouble afoot."

I nodded and gave a quick thanks before settling into one of the last row boats.

"Good luck," Trenton called out as he lowered us to the water.

*****

We had come across a damp cave behind a waterfall. I had a good feeling about this one. I made Manolo stand guard just behind the waterfall as we journeyed deeper.

It wasn't long until we came across an alter and on top of it was a coffin.

"This is it!" Ethan said.

"I've heard stories say that the chest wasn't any typical chest. That it was something to keep people away. What better than the potential of seeing a dead body?" Gibbons said behind me in husky, low voice.

Why they thought a few skeletons would keep pirates away, I had no idea. And I guess I didn't care.

I hurried to the coffin and tentatively slid the top off. The great stone landed with a thud.

What lay inside made my eyes widen. It was a decaying corpse. There was stringy grey hair that once formed a beard. His eyes... well I couldn't see them. I don't think I'd even want to see them. His garments were still in pretty good condition. I followed his arm, which was up near his head, and seen a gun. Gently taking it out of the corpse's hand I looked at the sigil that was stamped on the barrel. It was a skull with cross bones protruding out its nose and mouth. Deathman's symbol. Ethan leaned over me and gave a low whistle.

I peered closer and saw a crack in the bottom of his stone coffin.

"Help me move him. Get him out," I told the men.

Gibbons grabbed the end of Deathman while Lynch grabbed the head. They must have yanked too hard or handled the body too harshly because when they tossed him onto the ground the neck snapped. Lynch was left with the head in his hands.

He looked scared, actually scared, as he tossed the head away.

I started to press down on the stone until I found that one side started to lean down. Looking over I saw that the other side was sticking up.

"Lynch!" I called.

I had him hold down the bottom to as far as he could go and I went around to the side.

It was filled. Filled with gold, diamonds and jewelry.

"Boys! We found it!" I said excitedly.

"Gibbons! You and Manolo head back to the ship. Alert Saltman! He'll have you come back with empty barrels."

We waited a few hours before a pile of my men rushed into the cavern.

"Gentleman! We found the treasure of a lifetime!" I was met with loud cheers. "Let's wrap this up and head home!"

It didn't take us long to fill the barrels with treasure; not when most of my men were there to help.

"Succubus?" Ethan said behind me. I rolled my eyes at the name and turned to him. We were farther away from the men. They couldn't hear what we were saying.

"Yes?"

"Working with me wasn't so bad, now was it?"

I raised an eyebrow. "You lied about how long it would take to even get here. It only took us a few days to get past the storm. And you have a bet going on with my men about how long it will take to get to my bed."

He actually had the decency to look sheepish. "About the bet-"

I had a devilish idea. "What if we made a deal? I'll help you win that bet if you'll share your winnings. Half with me."

His eyes widened with surprise. "Help me win. Are you saying-"

"I don't have to actually sleep with you. All they need to see is me dragging you to my quarters, right?"

He frowned. He thought he'd actually get the bed. I almost burst out laughing.

"Fine. It's a deal," he finally said.

I nodded triumphantly and started to walk away.

"Wait! I'm not done. I wanted to talk to you about something else?"

I turned back around and gave him my full attention.

"I actually liked working with you. I know you didn't so much, but I did. I want to do a partnership. My pirates team up with yours. We can run our own ships, but we help each other find more treasure. I have leads on about a dozen more fortunes. We could really help each other."

I took a gold coin that was from the coffin and started to fiddle with it. "There's more treasure like this?"

"Yes," he affirmed.

Flipping the coin in the air, I shot him a grin. Catching the coin I said, "Well Ethan Earlman, looks like you have yourself a deal."

Four Years Later

I spied through my eyeglass Ethan's ship. He was having his turn steering his ship. I've noticed over the past few years how much he liked to steer his own ship. Smiling to myself, I folded up the eyeglass and slipped it into my belt.

"Ma'am," Trenton said from next me, steering our own ship. "You look happy."

I turned to him and gave him a wide grin. "Well, we are on our way to finding our third lot of treasure, are we not? There's much to be happy about."

"And then some," I heard him mumble as he looked at The Earlman, who was now passing by us.

It was typical of Ethan of to name his ship after himself.

I was about to respond to Trenton when I saw from the corner of my eye, Ethan swinging from his ship to mine. He was starting to remind me of this book I found a while back about a wild man in the jungle who swung from vines.

"Hello, love," Ethan said as he swaggered over and swept me into his arms.

I pushed him back with my hand. "Not now," I said in a teasing voice. "How much longer?"

"Ah. Business first, then play?"

I smirked. "Only if you give me what I want to hear."

"We'll be there in no less than a week."

I nodded. "You'll have to show me... on my map... that's in my office."

He nodded vigorously and led the way. Once we were behind closed doors, I took my chance and jumped. Locking my legs around his hips and my arms around his neck, I knocked him into my desk, causing papers and books to fall to the side.

"Careful! Those were expensive!" I scolded.

"Oh, you'll forgive me," he said while peppering kisses to my lips and neck.

I was starting to moan when he pulled away. "When will you let me hold you in front of our crew?"

"When you find that ring that you promised was in this next adventure."

"But what if it's not there?"

"Then you're going to have to go like every commoner and get one from a shop. If it comes down to that, it better be as big and beautiful as you said that this one is."

"Really?"

"No." And with that I shushed him with my kisses.

You're Still The One

By Chasity Tarantino

There was a knock on Adriel's hotel room door. She wasn't expecting anyone, so she didn't know who it could possibly be. She hadn't even ordered her dinner yet, so it couldn't be room service.

'That's odd,' she thought to herself as she got up off the bed and walked toward the door. She had just finished a showing of her clothing line in Paris. This had been a big deal for her, to finally show off her work in the fashion capital. She had wanted this since she was a little girl.

Honestly no one even knew she was back in town yet. Considering after her work was done in Paris, she decided she was going to take a month off and vacation there. She was so burnt out from working; she knew she deserved a little rest and relaxation. At least that's what she told everyone, but deep down she knew why she didn't really want to come back to LA. She just wasn't ready to face it.

Adriel made it to the door and looked out the peephole to see who her mystery guest was. Her heart dropped to her stomach and she slowly backed away from the door.

It was Mason.

'What is he doing here?' She thought frantically.

"Adriel, please open the door." He said evenly through the door.

Adriel pulled herself together, took a deep breath, and opened the door. "Mason, hi." She said praying her voice didn't betray how nervous she was.

He looked even better than he had the last time they had been together, his golden, shoulder length hair pushed back haphazardly as if he was constantly running his hands through it. His ice-blue eyes that she could get lost in were now boring into her own hazel ones. His perfectly sculpted cheek bones and luscious full lips made him look like an angel, except for the fact that he was dressed in all black. He was wearing a black V-neck shirt, black leather pants, and black boots; his signature silver chain bracelet hung loosely from his left wrist. His silver cross ring that haunted her glinted from his right hand. She could remember the feel of the cool metal on her skin all too well.

    He looked like perfection to Adriel but when she looked closely she noticed bags under his eyes, most likely from lack of sleep. Was he having trouble sleeping? Better yet what was he doing here?

    Mason and Adriel had dated for over a year. Adriel thought everything was going fine, she had really fallen for him. Mason was the drummer in a well-known rock band named 'The Hurricane' and had a reputation for being a player, but when she met him she didn't see that in him. He was a perfect gentleman, not to mention hilarious; he kept her smiling so much her cheeks hurt.

    Then right before she went to Paris, he dropped a bomb on her; he wanted to break up. He thought they were away from each other too much, that their schedules conflicted. At least that's what he told her, she thought there was someone else he was interested in considering they had always had grueling schedules and they had always worked around it. She flew to Paris the next week with a broken heart and a desperate urge to run away.

    "You look beautiful," were the first words out of his mouth.

    Her stomach churned violently. That wasn't fair.

    She was dressed in one of the summer dresses that she had designed herself. It was gray and fell to her ankles gracefully. It had a fitted bodice and hugged all her curves perfectly. She had always loved summer dresses, she thought they were the most comfortable thing you could wear and still look cute. Mason adored when she wore summer dresses; she was wearing one similar to the one she had on now when they first met. Her long auburn locks fell down over her back in soft curls. She hated putting her hair up, she adored her long locks that went past her bottom. Adriel was a petite beauty that never truly understood her effect on men when she walked into a room.

Together they were quite a pair, especially on the red carpet. They were a Hollywood 'it' couple and many were disappointed when they spilt.

"What are you doing here Mason?" She said sighing.

"I need to talk to you Adriel, can I come in?" He said rubbing his hands together.

That was something he only did when he was nervous, and only on rare occasions was Mason nervous.

She hesitated looking at him with questioning eyes.

"Please." He pleaded.

She sighed and stepped aside to let him in the room. He stepped into the room and she closed the door behind him.

"Nice room." He said as he looked around the room, then back at her.

She rolled her eyes; it was so typical of him to be calm and casual while her insides went haywire.

"Mason what did you come here for?" She repeated her question as she sat down on the bed.

He walked over to her and looked down into her eyes. His beautiful eyes that seemed to look right through her soul.

"I came to tell you that I made a big mistake." He said softly, still gazing into her eyes, "I should've never let you walk out the door that night. I knew I screwed up as soon as you were gone."

Her heart clenched, was this really happening?

"Please don't do this. It's not fair." She muttered.

She wanted to believe him so bad and forget all of this had even happened, but she just couldn't. He had really hurt her and she still questioned his motives for breaking up with her in the first place.

He knelt down in front of her and grabbed her left hand with his right. "Please Adriel, you have to believe me. I can't stop thinking about you. I was so wrong to believe this wasn't real. I need you Adriel." He was practically begging, she could hear the pain in his voice.

"Are you really sitting here telling me this? What has happened Mason? Did you get tired of your little fling already?" She asked sarcastically.

She was so sure that there was another girl. She thought his 'playboy' reputation had finally reared its ugly head and it sure had bitten her.

"No, why would you think that? I've missed you like crazy. There was no fling. What are you talking about?" He said his eyes widening in surprise.

"Then why did you end it? Remember it was you who wanted to break up, not me. I figured you found a new girl." She said reminding him that it was indeed his doing that caused this.

"No, there wasn't a new girl. Are you out of your mind? I know I made a huge mistake. I know I messed up, but I was so afraid of the idea of a commitment that I ran away. I'm so ashamed of how I handled it and I miss you like crazy." He said.

"I don't understand, if that's how you felt, why did you wait until now to tell me?" She asked confusion written across her face.

He had ended their relationship, out of nowhere; she needed to know exactly why so she didn't make the same mistake twice. Not to mention the fact that he waited a month to tell her that he wanted to get back together.

"I thought you stayed in Paris because you didn't want to see me and honestly I had too much pride to admit I was wrong, but I was wrong. We belong together, Adriel. I love you and I never stopped loving you."

She didn't respond at first, of course that's what she wanted to hear. She wanted him back so bad that she had dreams of him coming back to her, but she had a gnawing feeling eating away at her gut. What if he hurt her again and left her because he got bored? Could she really go through this again?

He stared at her in anticipation. He could see the doubt in her eyes, and his heart was racing at such a high speed he thought it might just fly right out of his chest. How could he convince her that he needed her in his life?

"Adriel, please I am telling you the truth. I should have told you how I really felt ages ago. I was scared of how strong my feelings were. I knew if you left me, I'd be nothing. So I was a coward and left first. I'm not proud of it, but I am trying to make it right, love." He pleaded reaching up to push a strand of hair that had fallen in front of her face, back behind her ear.

She looked into his eyes for a minute before looking down at her hands. She needed to be strong and get this out, but if she kept looking in those beautiful blue eyes she would never get him out of her room. "Mason I don't know what to tell you." She sighed still looking at her hands, "You're too late. I met someone in Paris."

Mason jerked back as if she had slapped him. "What? Who?" He asked rather loudly.

"His name is Garrett, he's a model. He worked in one of my shows." She said avoiding his eyes.

His eyes widened, he waited too long, and it took a minute for that to seep in. His veins felt like they were filling with ice at the realization that he had lost her. He knew he should have gone after her.

"How did you know I was back anyway?" She asked meeting his eyes finally.

"The show was all over the tabloids, so were the theories as to why you stayed in Paris. You know the usual; pregnancy, drug addiction, the typical downward spiral." He explained, "I called Stacy and begged her to tell me when you were coming back."

Stacy was her publicist and thought that she and Mason were perfect together, but Adriel had given the strict order not to reveal when she was coming back to anyone. Apparently Mason was not just anyone.

"Don't be mad at her, she didn't want to tell me, trust me. I made a bit of a scene for her, I'm afraid."

"It's fine. Mason, I really think you should go." She said standing up.

"That's it? Garrett has your heart now?" He said the name 'Garrett' like it was a disease.

"I'm sorry, but I've moved on. This was not my doing, Mason." She said wearily, walking over to the door and opening it. She leaned against it; her hand clutching the doorknob.

Her stomach was tightly knotted; she just needed to get him out of here before she gave in.

Mason sighed, "I never wanted it to end like this Adriel. I never wanted it to end period."

"Please just go." She said motioning to the hallway.

He walked out the door and looked back at her; the pain was evident in his eyes. "Adriel…" he began, but was cut off when the hotel door slammed closed in his face.

Inside the hotel room Adriel moved numbly toward the bed before collapsing on it, attempting to take deep breaths as the tears ran down her cheeks. She couldn't even begin to explain to herself why she had turned him away.

A few nights later Adriel and Garrett were at a party hosted by an elite supermodel named Camilla, who was a close friend of Garrett. Adriel didn't want to be there to begin with, let alone be there with Garrett. She liked Garrett; he was a nice guy and was easy on the eyes. He had chin length brunette hair; very beautiful hazel eyes; and of course he had amazing bone structure, typical of a runway model. However it seemed being with Garrett was a lot easier when she thought that Mason moved on. Now his words were constantly flying around in her head, weighing heavily on her.

Garret seemed to be having the time of his life; glass of champagne in hand, dancing around the room with anyone within his grasp.

Adriel sighed, closed her eyes, and rubbed at her temples in an attempt to alleviate the pressure that had gathered in her head.

She suddenly felt someone's gaze on her. She looked up and did a quick scan of the room.

Sure enough she locked eyes with a familiar icy blue gaze. Mason.

She grabbed a glass of champagne off the tray of a waiter walking by and quickly turned around, bringing her gaze back to Garrett. She couldn't think any more about how good Mason looked, or how what he said was so right. She downed the flute of champagne, trying to fight the desperate urge to run into Mason's arms.

Her self-control failed and she turned her head just enough to see where he was standing, but he wasn't there. She turned her whole body around and searched the room but he was nowhere to be found. Had she imagined him standing there?

'Good lord I need to get a grip.' She thought to herself.

A few minutes later she grew tired of watching Garrett mingle and act foolishly, so she made her way to the bathroom at the back of the suite where the party was being held. She was going to use the bathroom and then leave this overrated party. Garrett could fend for himself, since it seemed he already was.

When Adriel opened the bathroom door after using the restroom, she gasped. Mason was standing there blocking her way out. She stepped back as he moved into the bathroom with her, closed the door behind him and then he turned to face her.

"Mason what…?" her question was lost as his lips crashed against hers.

She tensed at first, not expecting the kiss, then she quickly gave in to kissing him back.

It felt so right, it felt like home. He felt like home, this was the man whose arms she was supposed to be in.

Could she really allow herself to fall again?

She pulled away from his eager lips taking a breath. "Mason stop. What about Garrett?" She muttered in his ear as he kissed her neck, never once letting her leave his grip.

One hand was firmly placed on her hip, the other on the back of her neck, bringing her closer to him. Their faces were only inches apart. "You're not his. You're mine. Always have been, always will be." He replied with a look of determination and desire she had never seen before.

"Mason, I…." again she was interrupted.

"I know you don't want him. Please, I know I hurt you; I deserved what happened, but Adriel we belong together. I love you."

Right in that moment, looking into his eyes, she knew he was telling the truth. They did belong together. She nodded her head once. "I love you too." She responded as a smile slowly appeared on her face.

He beamed back at her. "Good because my life would suck without you."